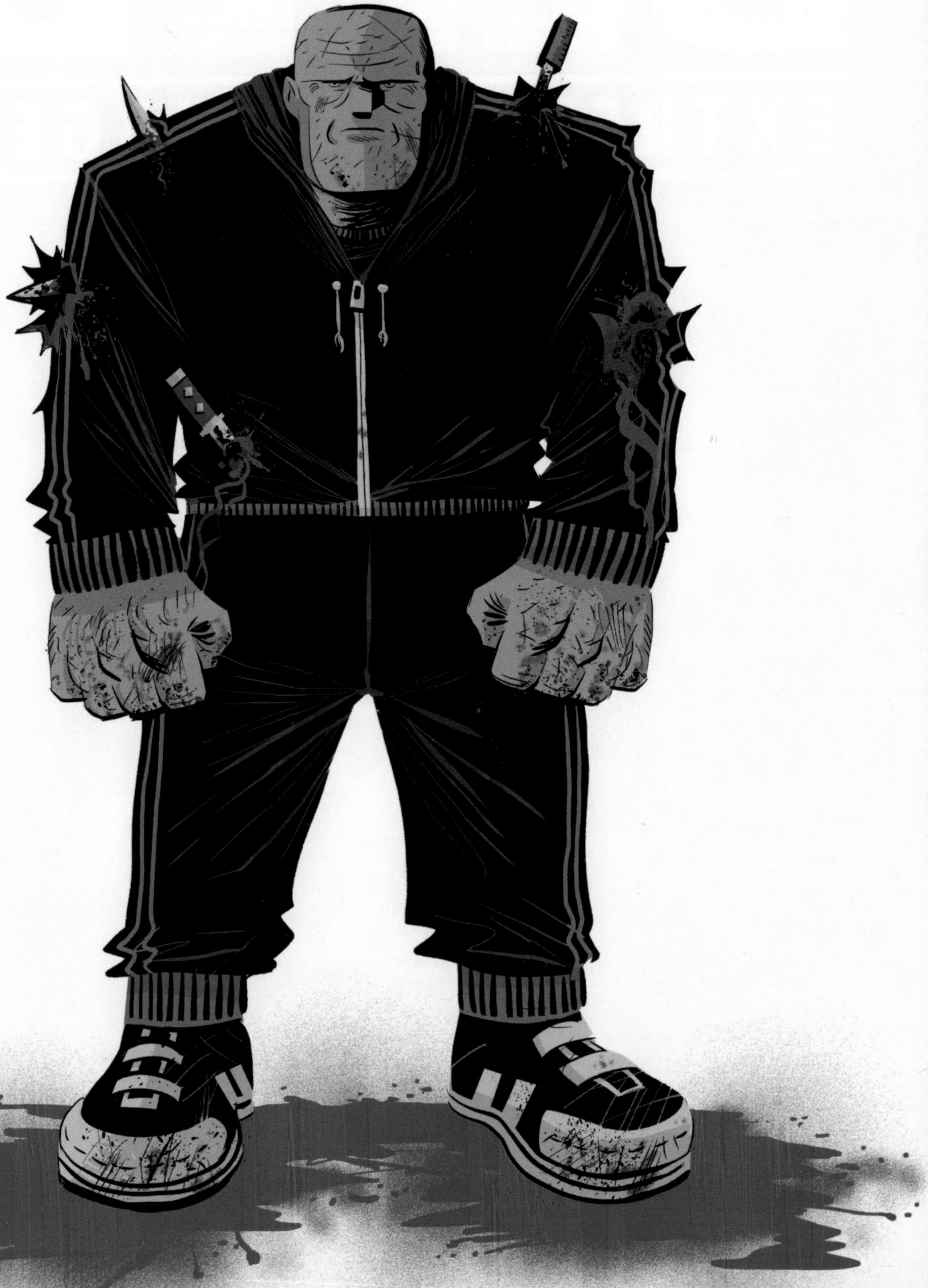

# VICTOR SANTOS
# UNTIL MY KNUCKLES BLEED
## EXTREMELY DAMAGED
### PART 1

# THE 90s

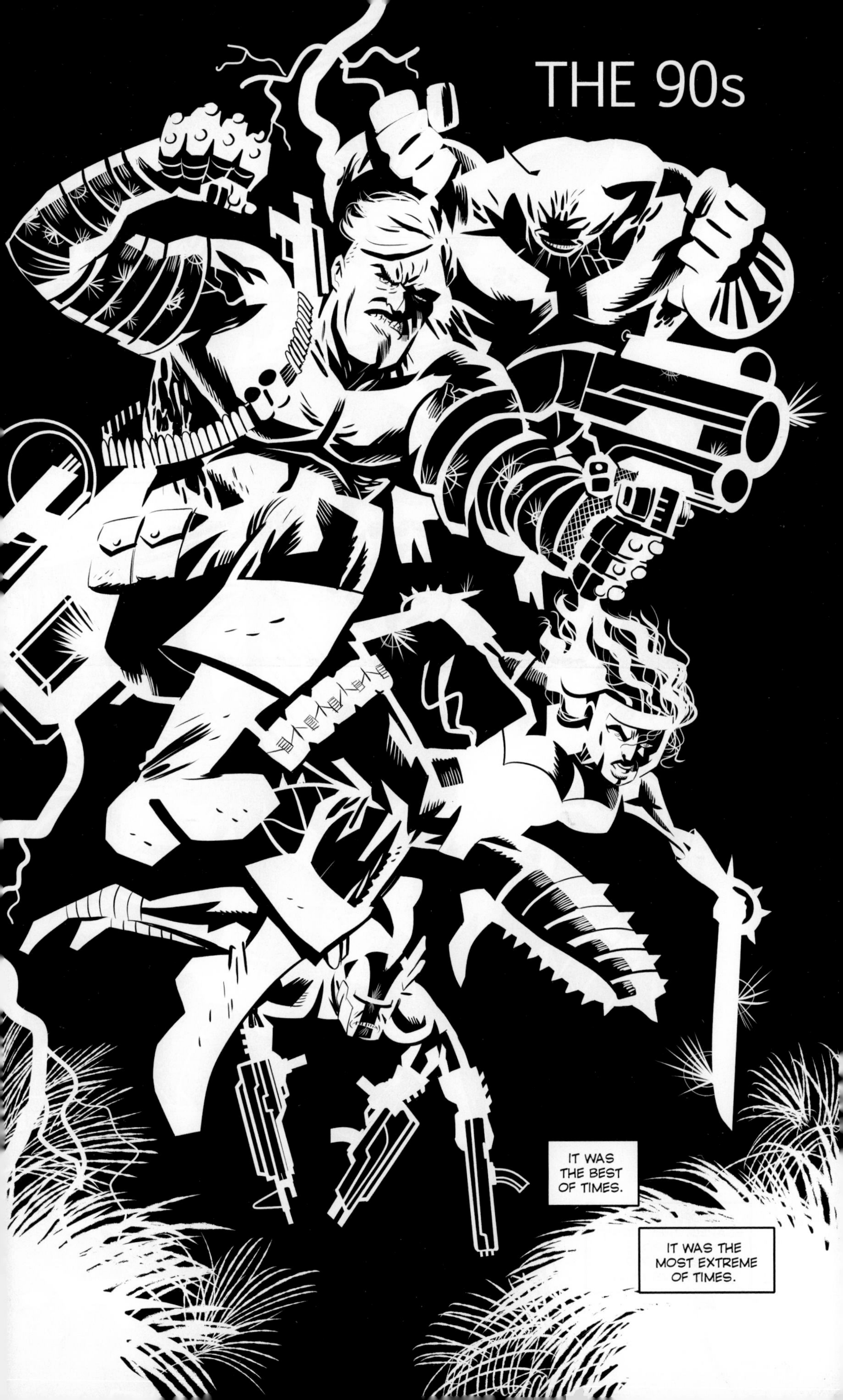
IT WAS THE BEST OF TIMES.
IT WAS THE MOST EXTREME OF TIMES.

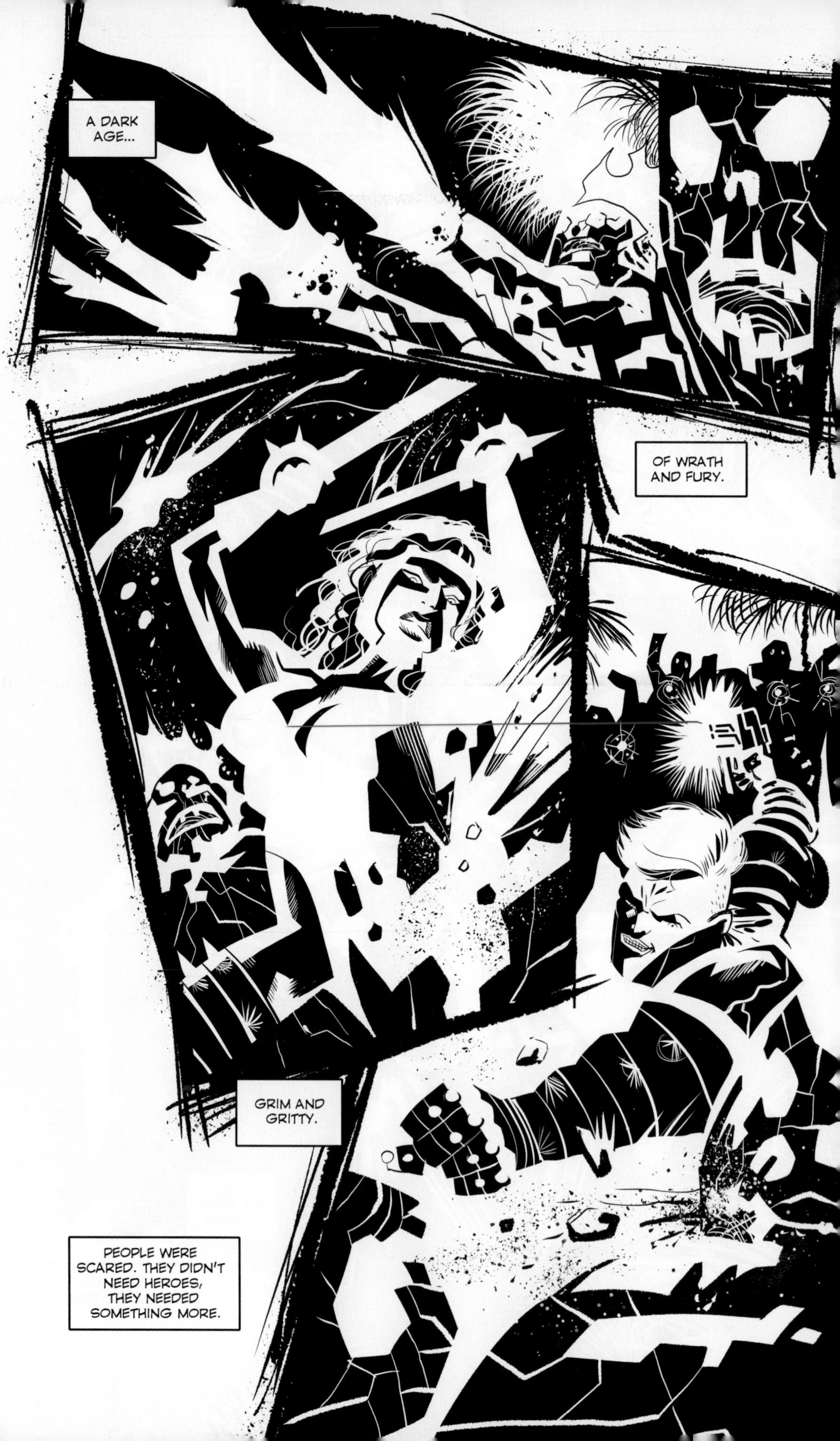

A DARK AGE...
OF WRATH AND FURY.
GRIM AND GRITTY.
PEOPLE WERE SCARED. THEY DIDN'T NEED HEROES, THEY NEEDED SOMETHING MORE.

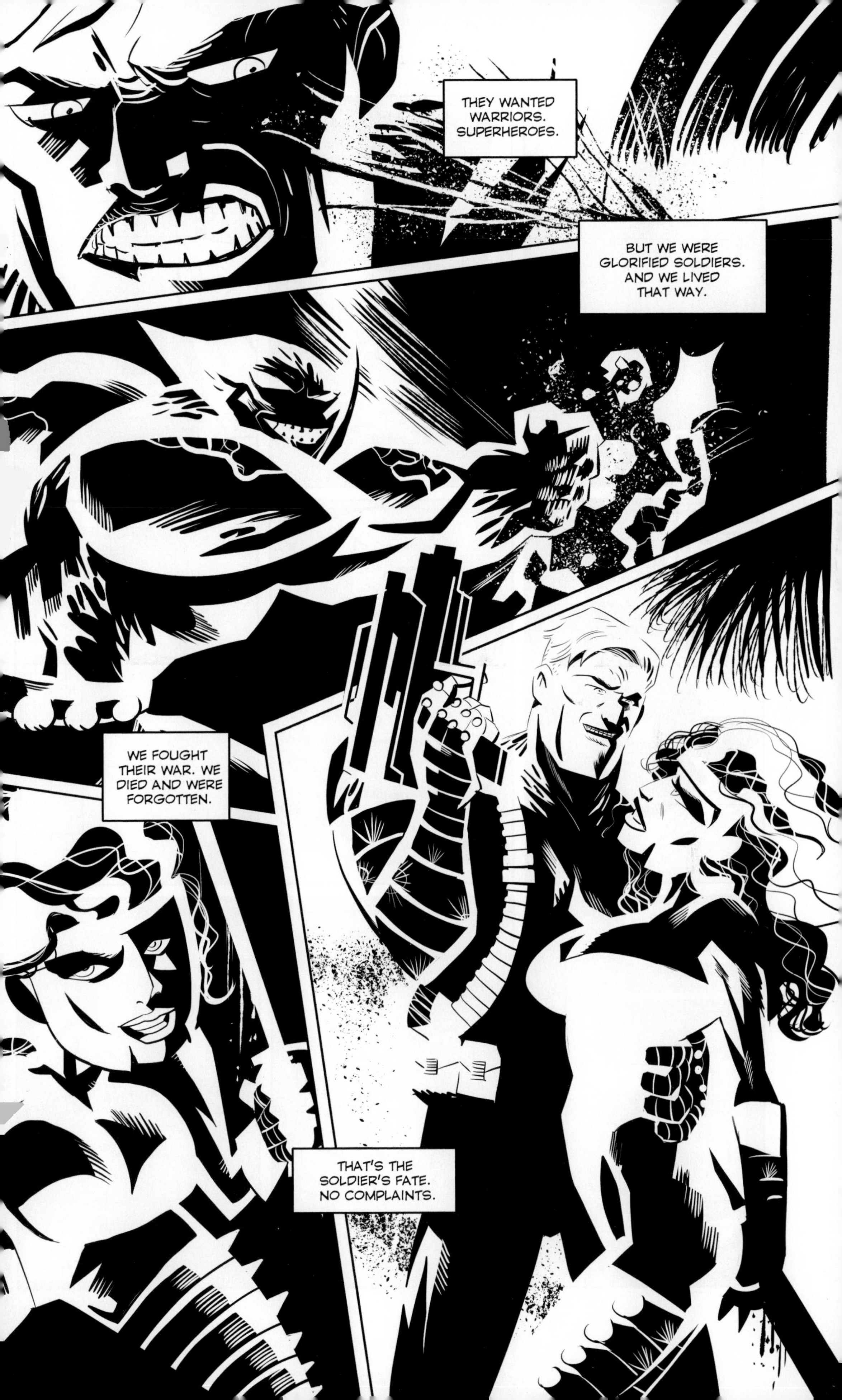
THEY WANTED WARRIORS. SUPERHEROES.
BUT WE WERE GLORIFIED SOLDIERS. AND WE LIVED THAT WAY.
WE FOUGHT THEIR WAR. WE DIED AND WERE FORGOTTEN.
THAT'S THE SOLDIER'S FATE. NO COMPLAINTS.

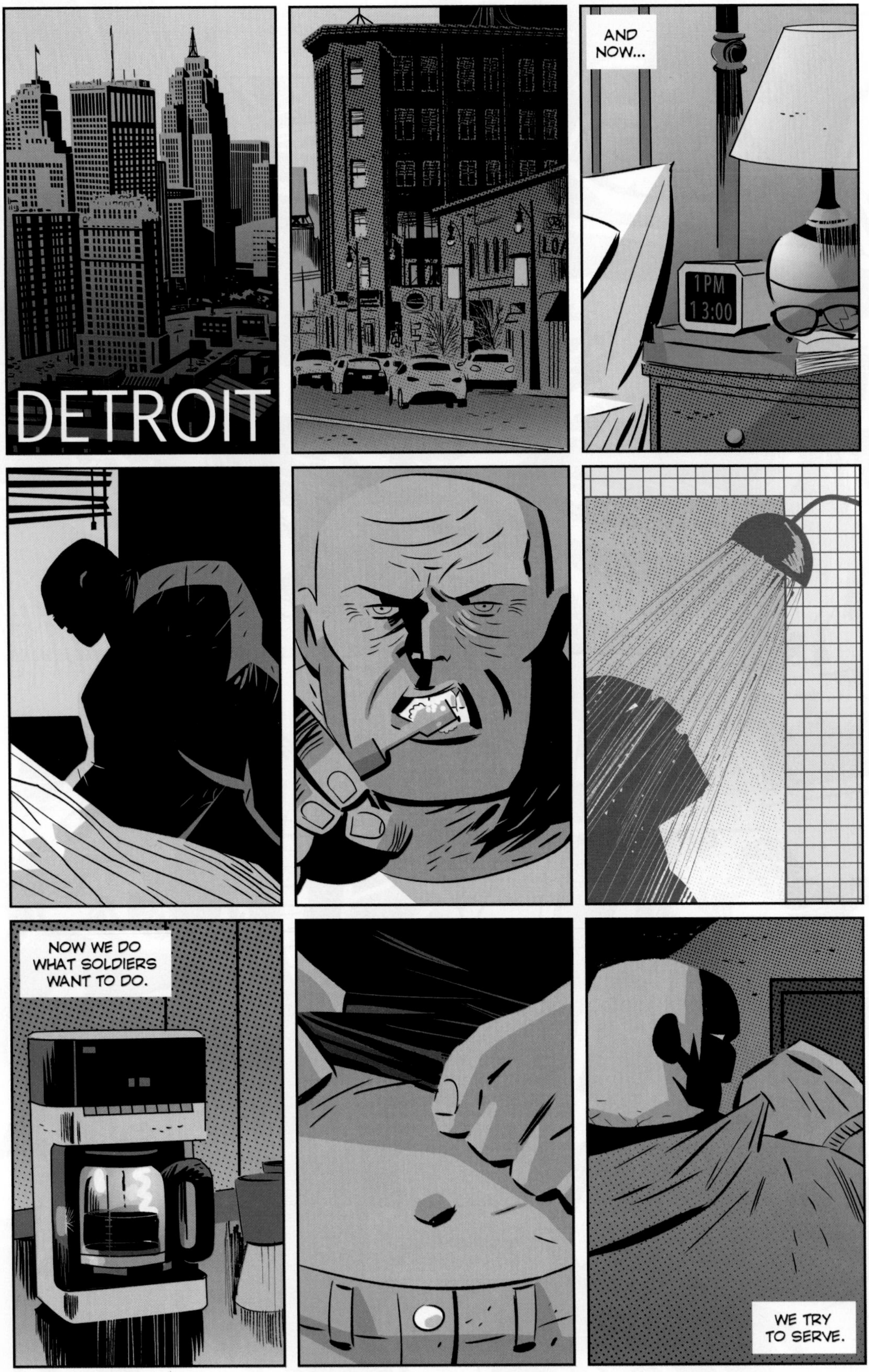
DETROIT
AND NOW...
1PM
13:00
NOW WE DO WHAT SOLDIERS WANT TO DO.
WE TRY TO SERVE.

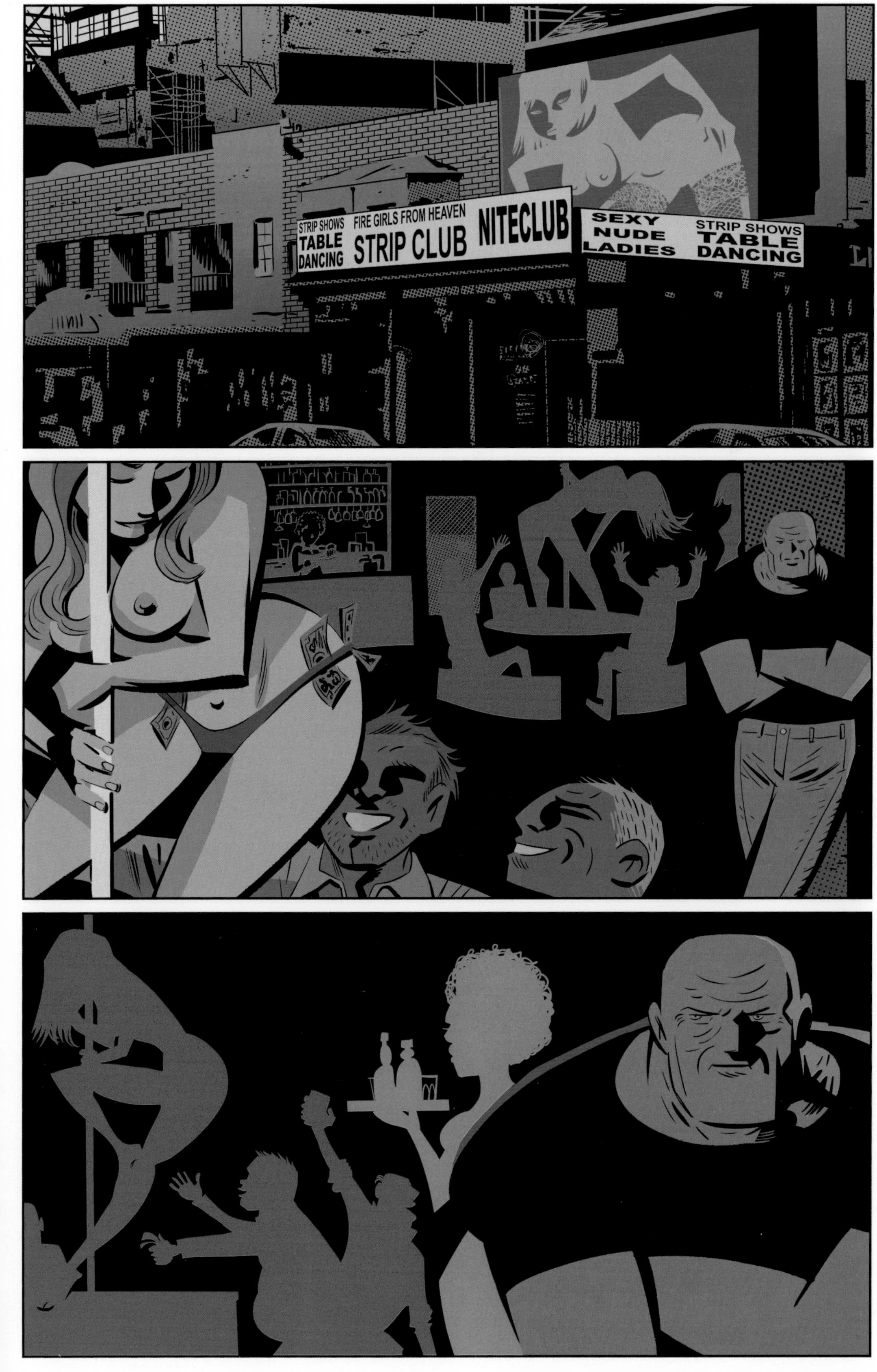
STRIP SHOWS
TABLE
DANCING
FIRE GIRLS FROM HEAVEN
STRIP CLUB
NITECLUB
SEXY
NUDE
LADIES
STRIP SHOWS
TABLE
DANCING

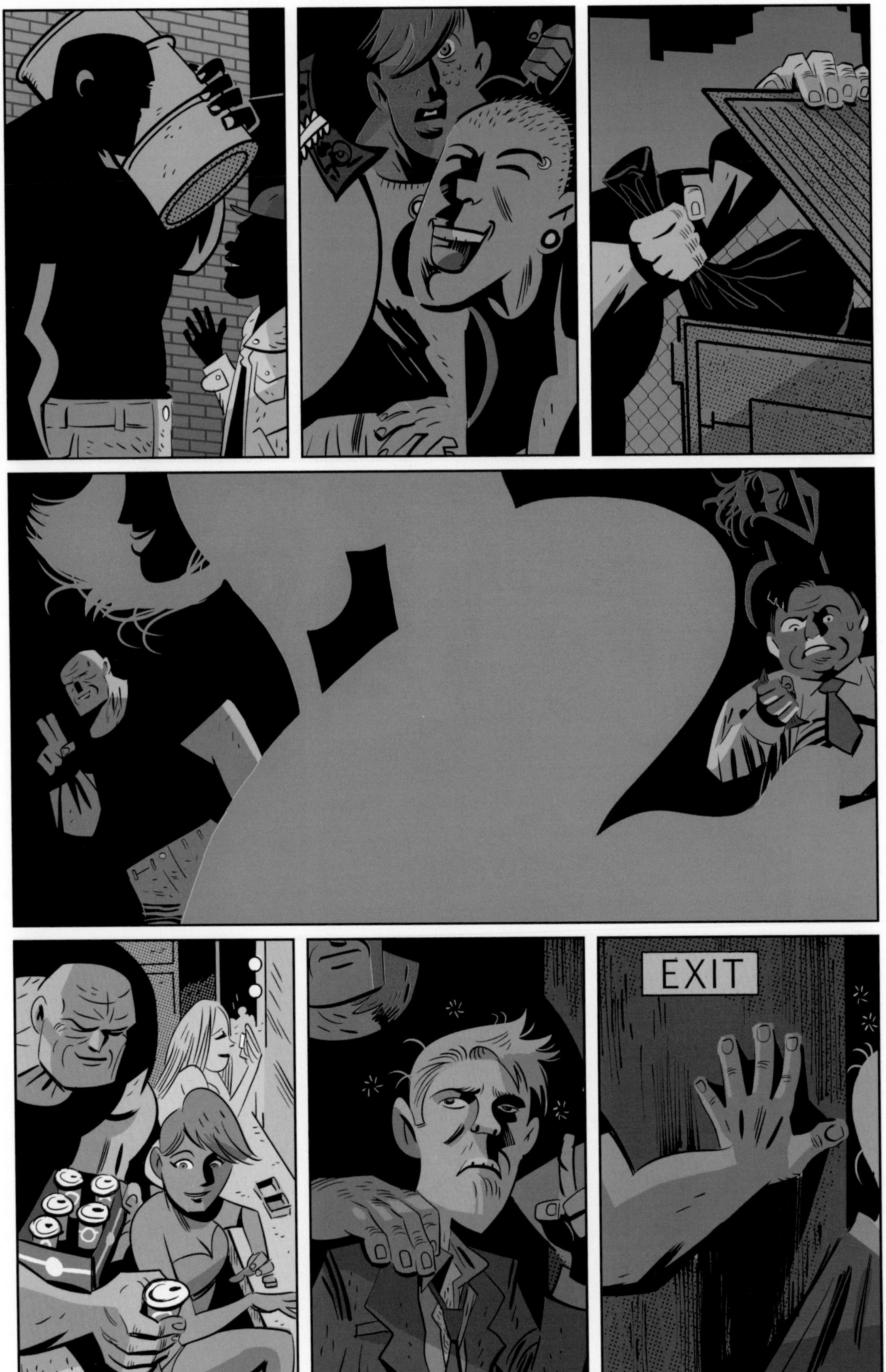

EXIT

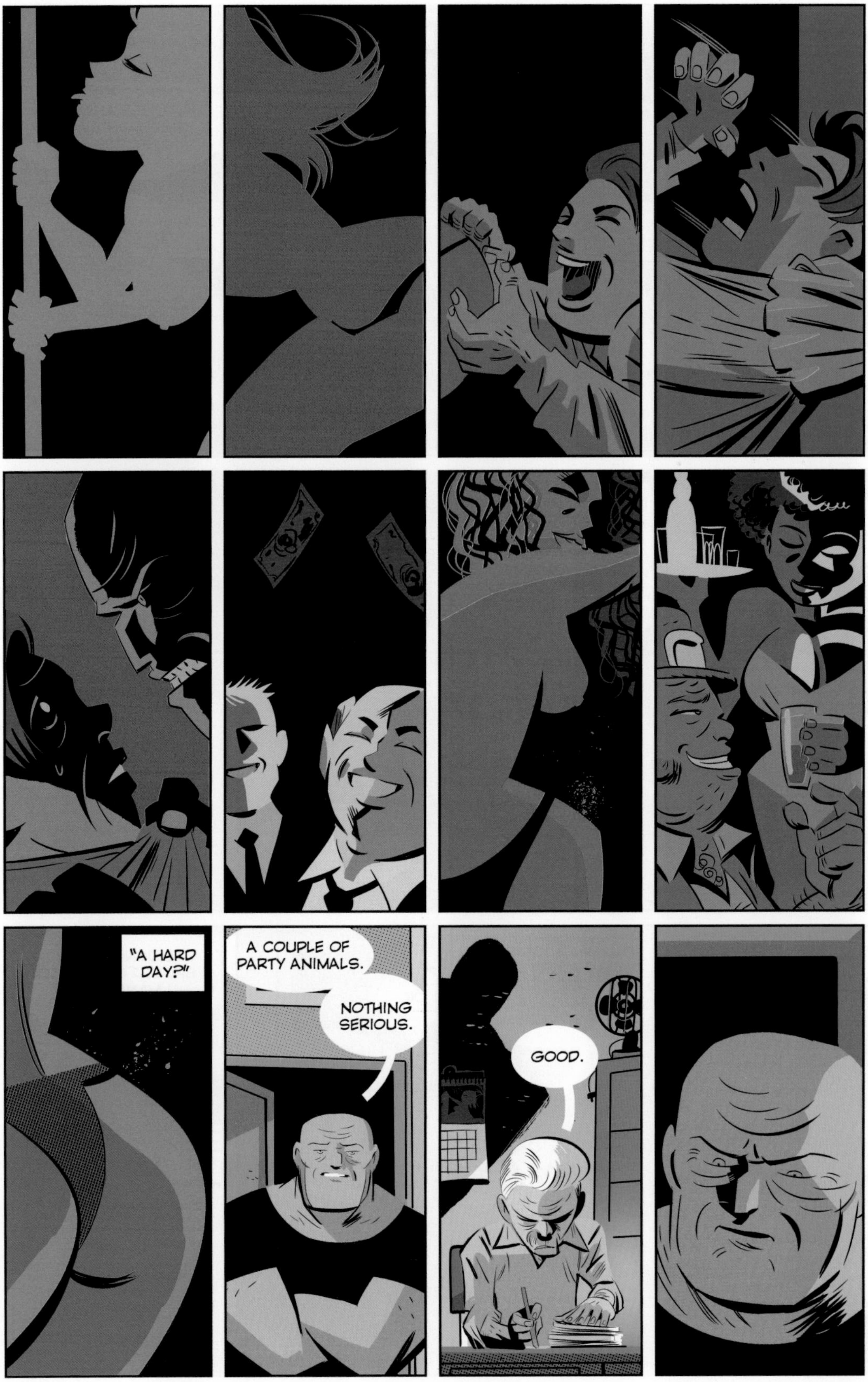
"A HARD DAY?"
A COUPLE OF PARTY ANIMALS.
NOTHING SERIOUS.
GOOD.

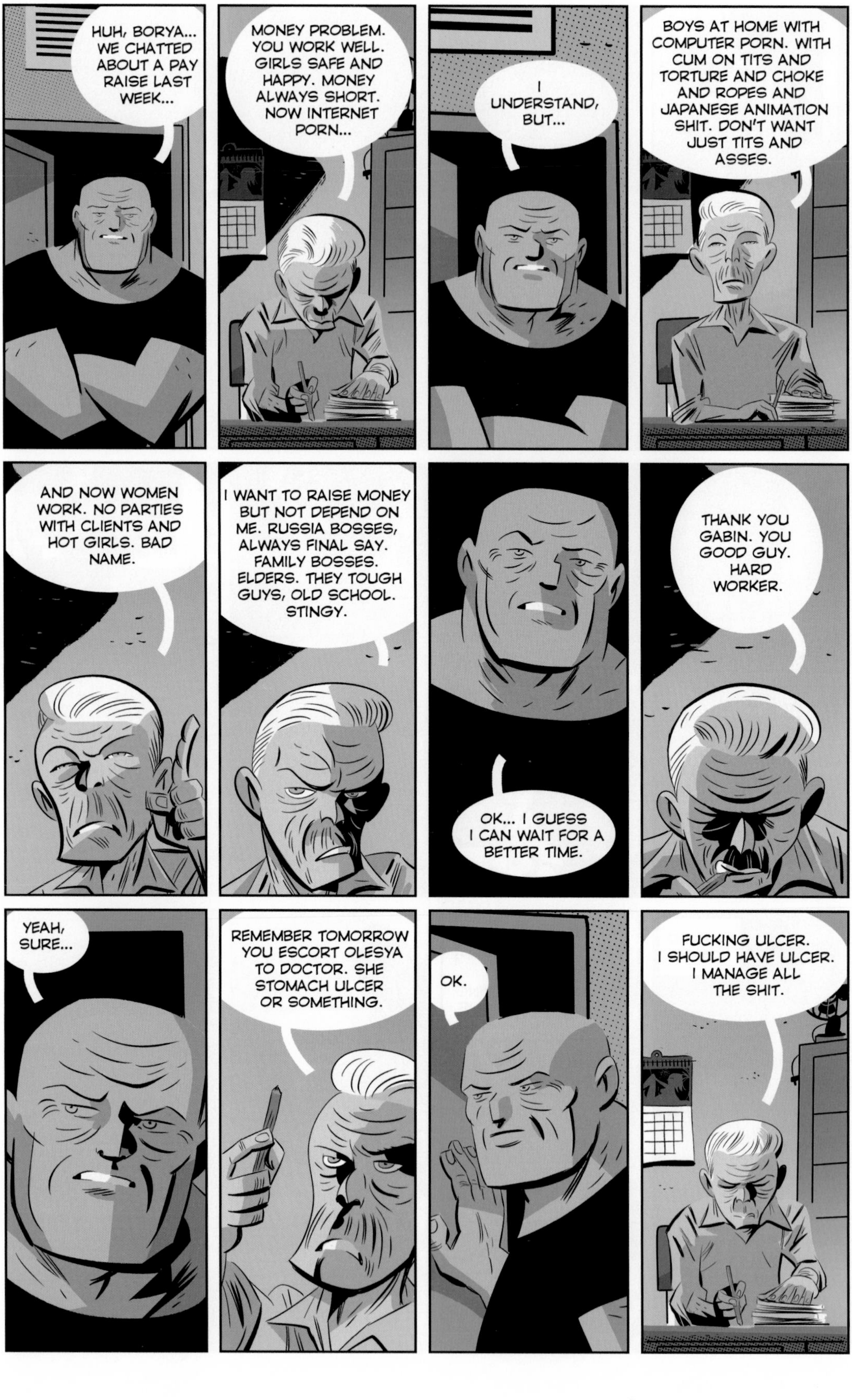
HUH, BORYA... WE CHATTED ABOUT A PAY RAISE LAST WEEK...
MONEY PROBLEM. YOU WORK WELL. GIRLS SAFE AND HAPPY. MONEY ALWAYS SHORT. NOW INTERNET PORN...
I UNDERSTAND, BUT...
BOYS AT HOME WITH COMPUTER PORN. WITH CUM ON TITS AND TORTURE AND CHOKE AND ROPES AND JAPANESE ANIMATION SHIT. DON'T WANT JUST TITS AND ASSES.
AND NOW WOMEN WORK. NO PARTIES WITH CLIENTS AND HOT GIRLS. BAD NAME.
I WANT TO RAISE MONEY BUT NOT DEPEND ON ME. RUSSIA BOSSES, ALWAYS FINAL SAY. FAMILY BOSSES. ELDERS. THEY TOUGH GUYS, OLD SCHOOL. STINGY.
OK... I GUESS I CAN WAIT FOR A BETTER TIME.
THANK YOU GABIN. YOU GOOD GUY. HARD WORKER.
YEAH, SURE...
REMEMBER TOMORROW YOU ESCORT OLESYA TO DOCTOR. SHE STOMACH ULCER OR SOMETHING.
OK.
FUCKING ULCER. I SHOULD HAVE ULCER. I MANAGE ALL THE SHIT.

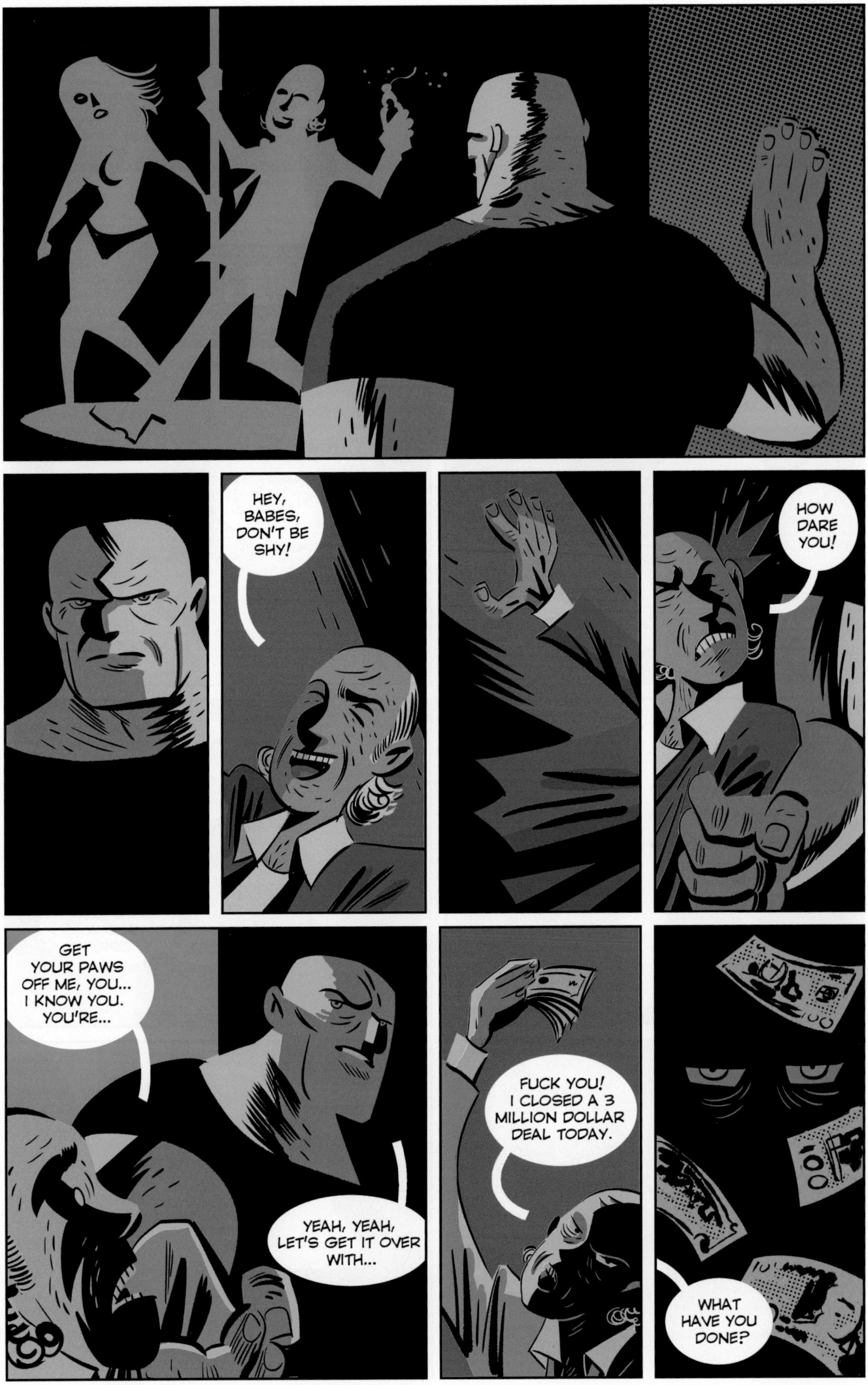
HEY, BABES, DON'T BE SHY!
HOW DARE YOU!
GET YOUR PAWS OFF ME, YOU... I KNOW YOU. YOU'RE...
YEAH, YEAH, LET'S GET IT OVER WITH...
FUCK YOU! I CLOSED A 3 MILLION DOLLAR DEAL TODAY.
WHAT HAVE YOU DONE?

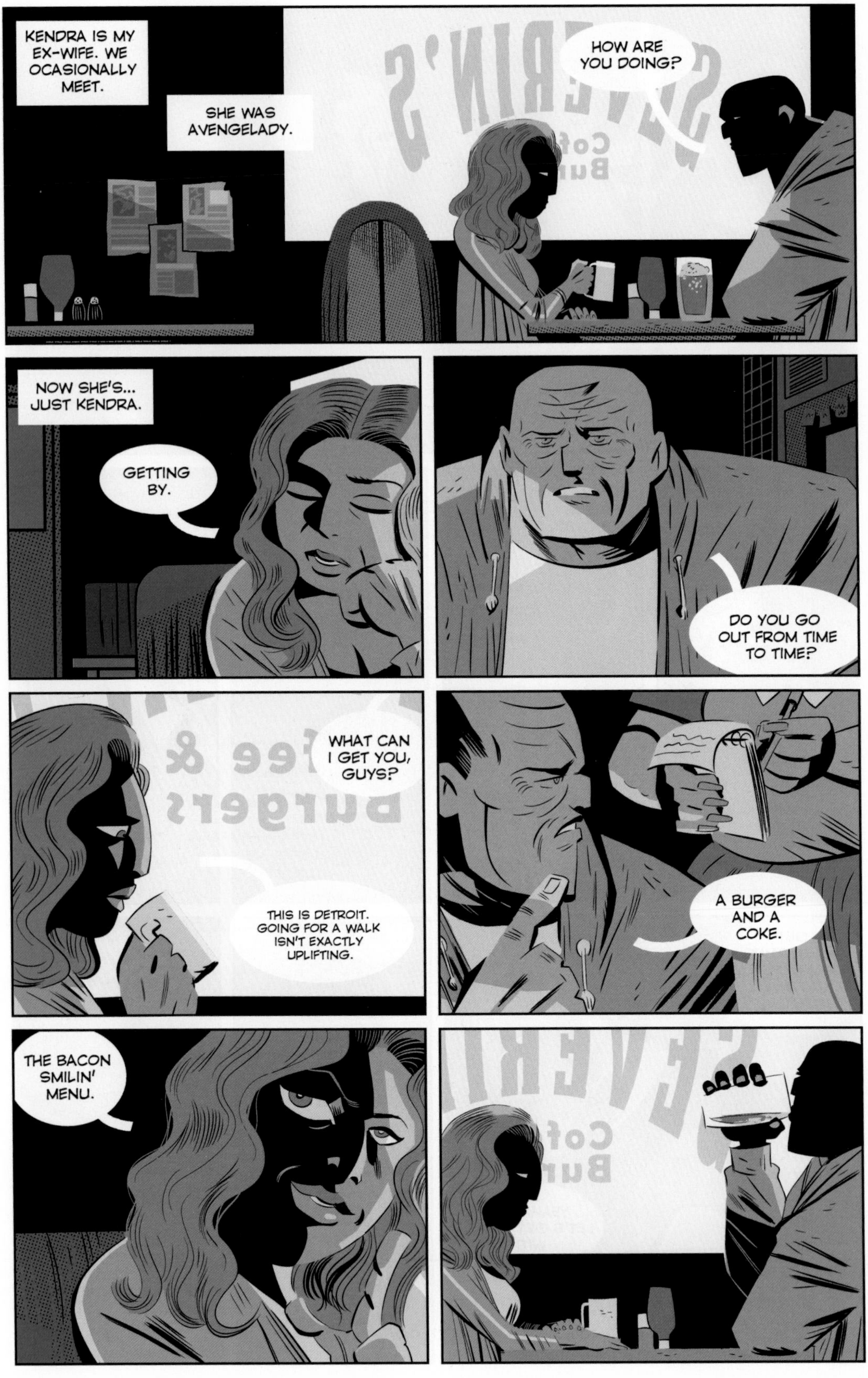

KENDRA IS MY EX-WIFE. WE OCASIONALLY MEET.
SHE WAS AVENGELADY.
HOW ARE YOU DOING?
NOW SHE'S... JUST KENDRA.
GETTING BY.
DO YOU GO OUT FROM TIME TO TIME?
THIS IS DETROIT. GOING FOR A WALK ISN'T EXACTLY UPLIFTING.
WHAT CAN I GET YOU, GUYS?
A BURGER AND A COKE.
THE BACON SMILIN' MENU.

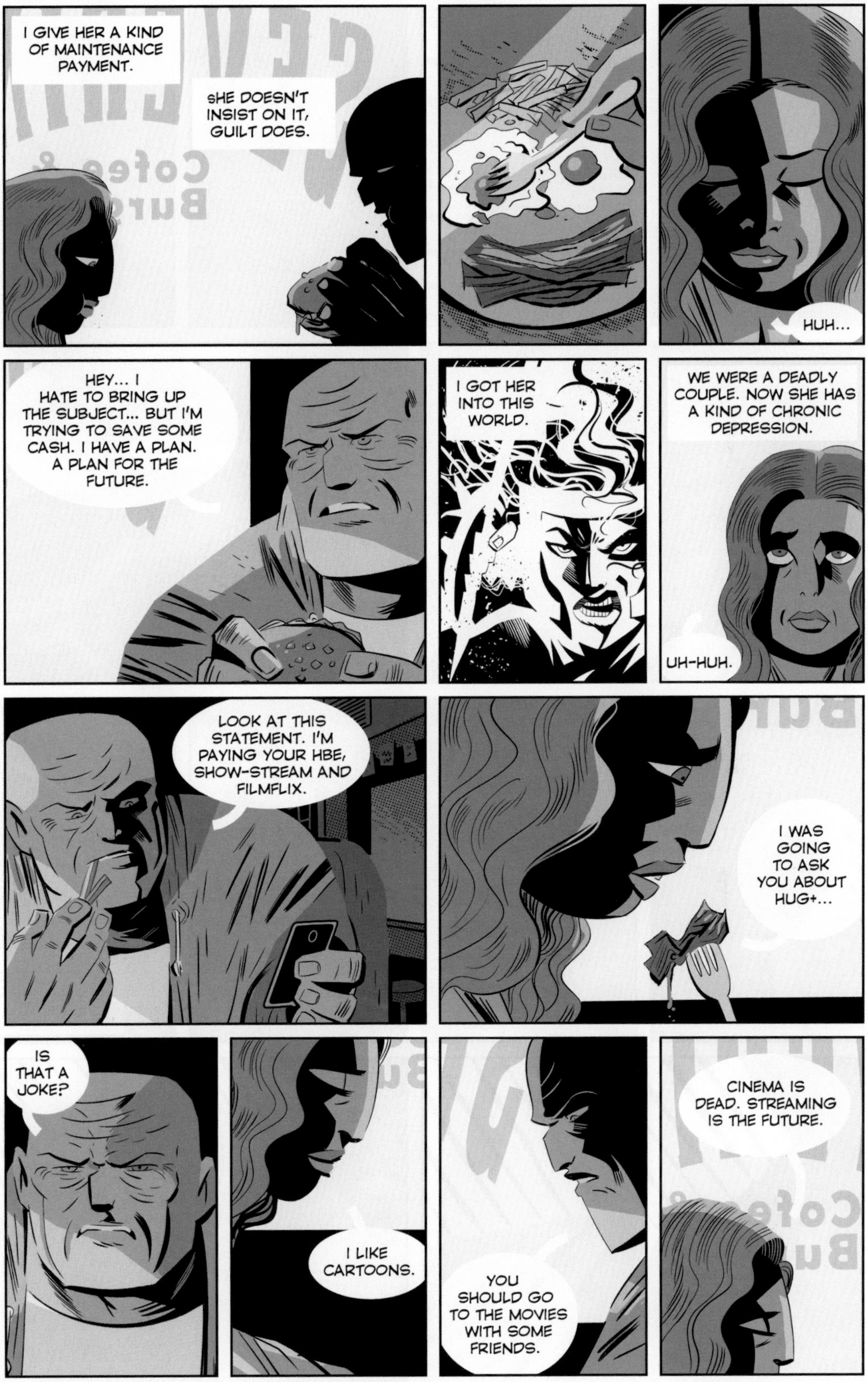

I GIVE HER A KIND OF MAINTENANCE PAYMENT.
SHE DOESN'T INSIST ON IT, GUILT DOES.
HUH...
HEY... I HATE TO BRING UP THE SUBJECT... BUT I'M TRYING TO SAVE SOME CASH. I HAVE A PLAN. A PLAN FOR THE FUTURE.
I GOT HER INTO THIS WORLD.
WE WERE A DEADLY COUPLE. NOW SHE HAS A KIND OF CHRONIC DEPRESSION.
UH-HUH.
LOOK AT THIS STATEMENT. I'M PAYING YOUR HBE, SHOW-STREAM AND FILMFLIX.
I WAS GOING TO ASK YOU ABOUT HUG+...
IS THAT A JOKE?
I LIKE CARTOONS.
YOU SHOULD GO TO THE MOVIES WITH SOME FRIENDS.
CINEMA IS DEAD. STREAMING IS THE FUTURE.

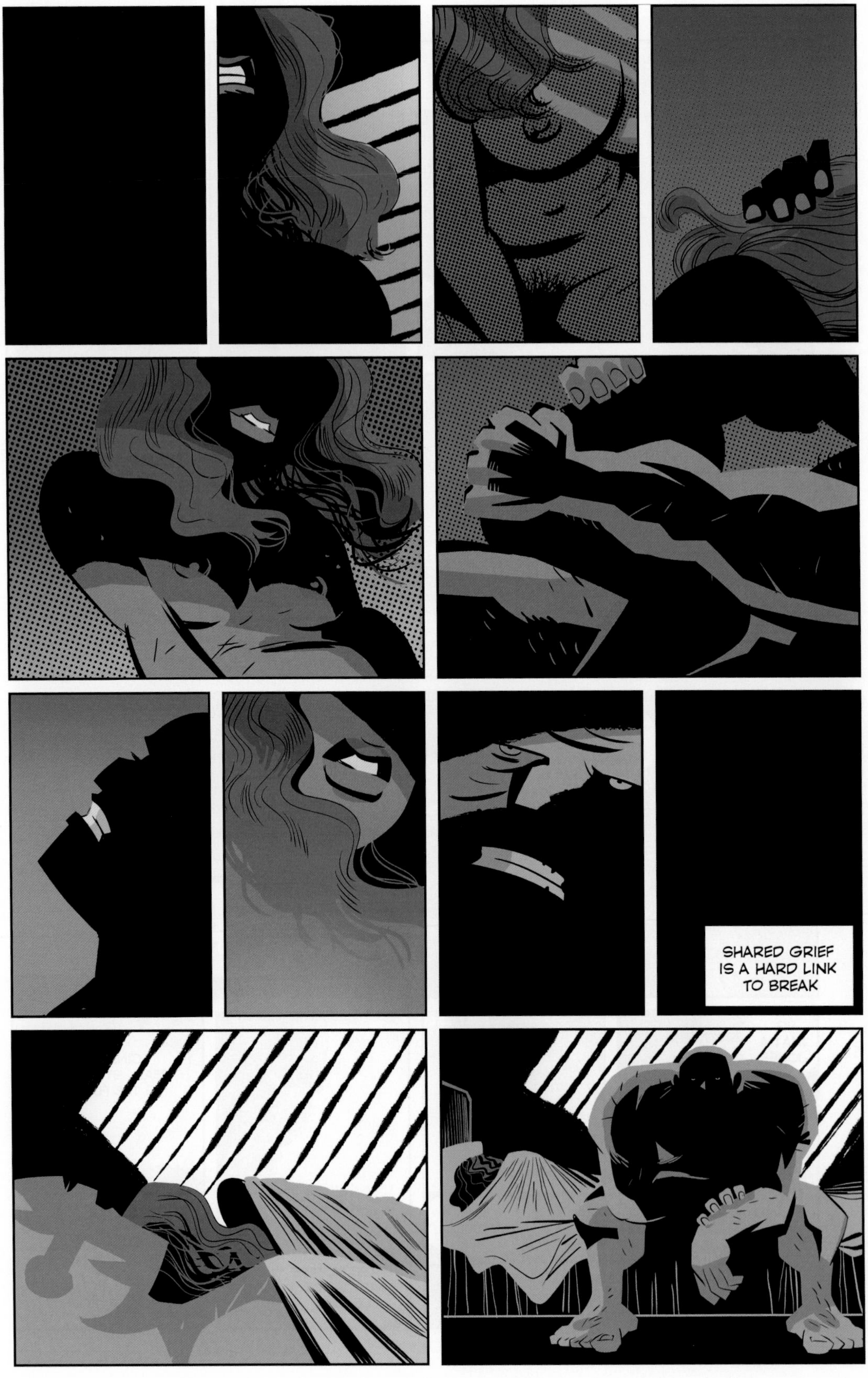
SHARED GRIEF
IS A HARD LINK
TO BREAK

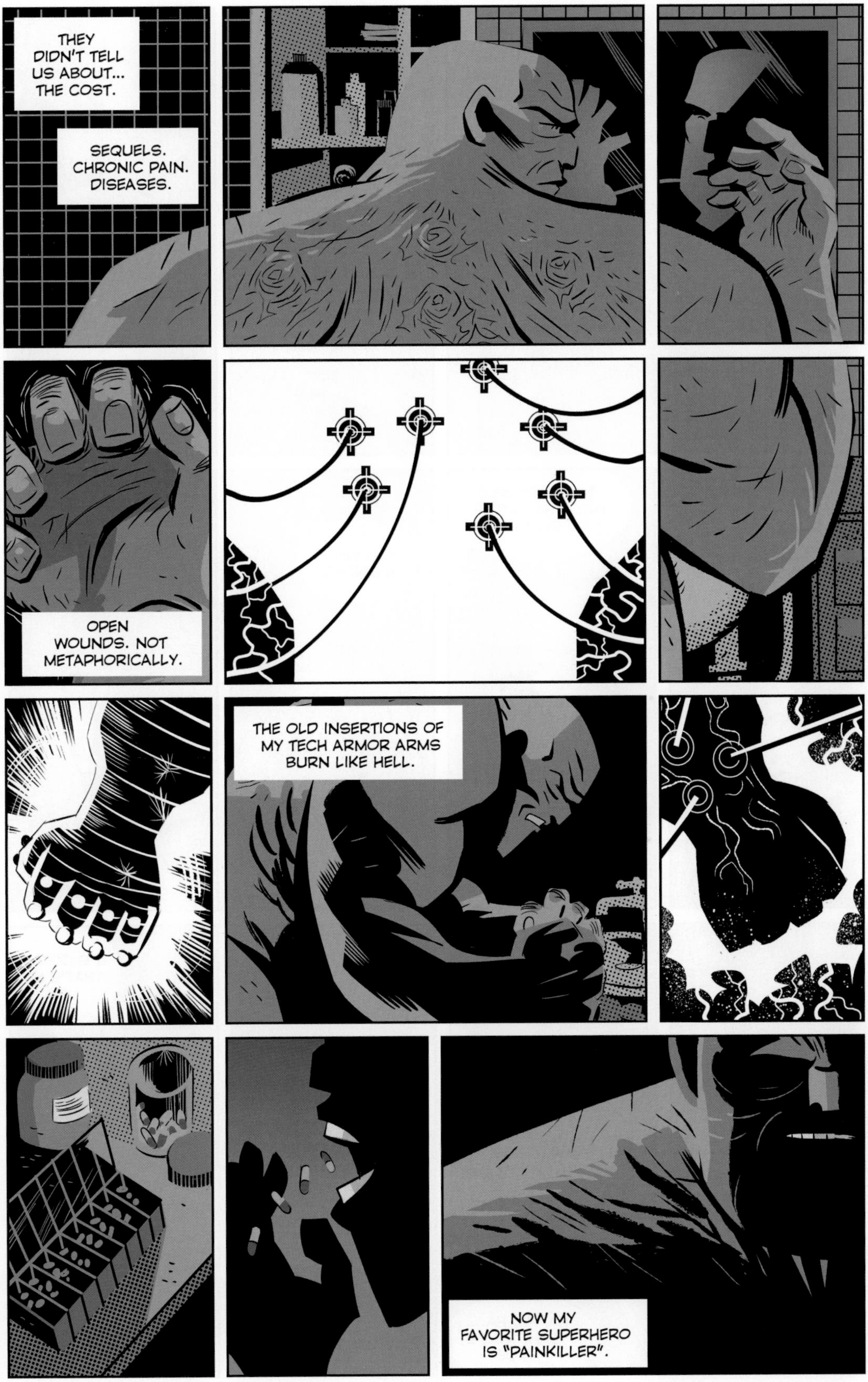
THEY DIDN'T TELL US ABOUT... THE COST.
SEQUELS. CHRONIC PAIN. DISEASES.
OPEN WOUNDS. NOT METAPHORICALLY.
THE OLD INSERTIONS OF MY TECH ARMOR ARMS BURN LIKE HELL.
NOW MY FAVORITE SUPERHERO IS "PAINKILLER".

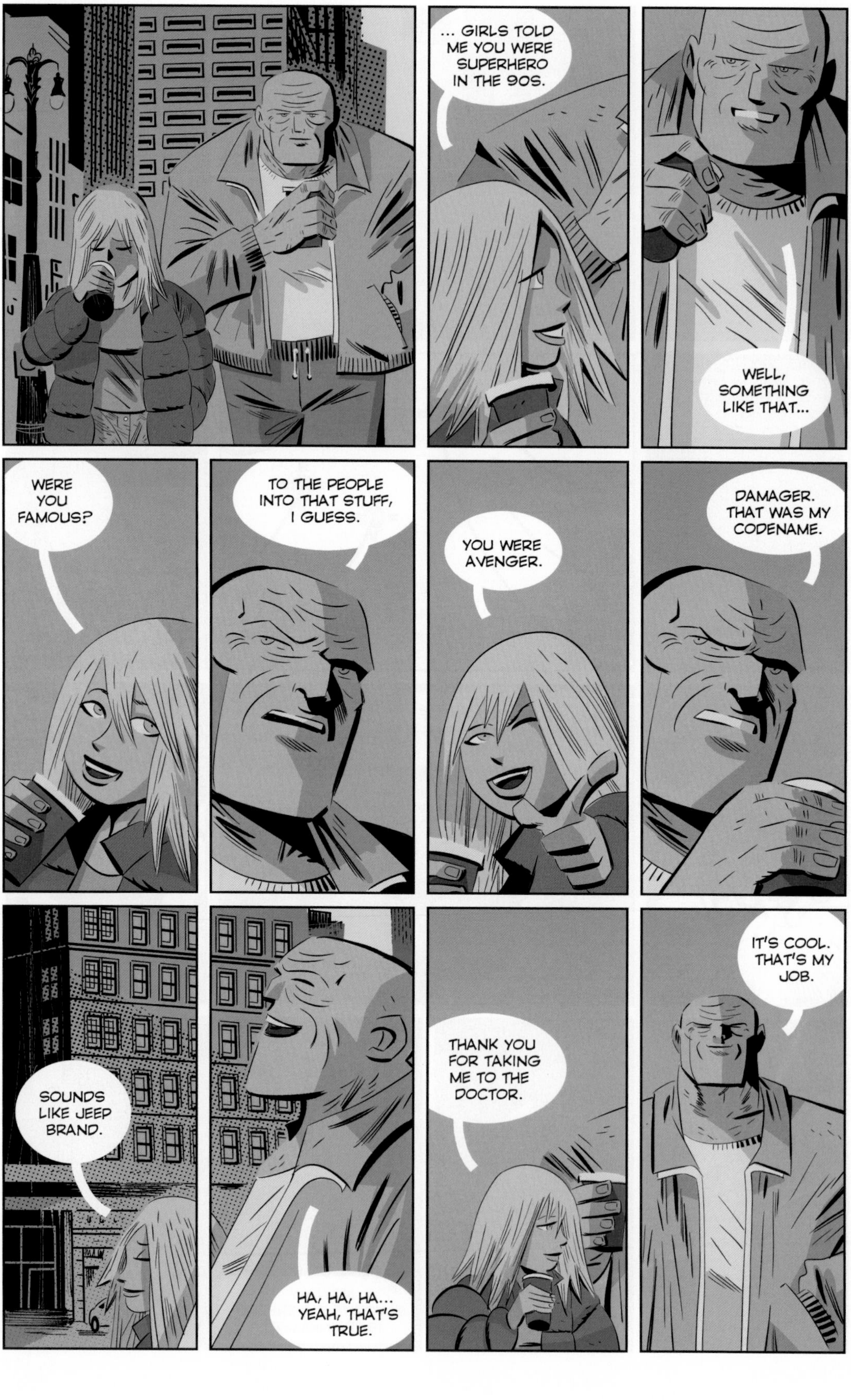

... GIRLS TOLD ME YOU WERE SUPERHERO IN THE 90S.
WELL, SOMETHING LIKE THAT...
WERE YOU FAMOUS?
TO THE PEOPLE INTO THAT STUFF, I GUESS.
YOU WERE AVENGER.
DAMAGER. THAT WAS MY CODENAME.
SOUNDS LIKE JEEP BRAND.
HA, HA, HA... YEAH, THAT'S TRUE.
THANK YOU FOR TAKING ME TO THE DOCTOR.
IT'S COOL. THAT'S MY JOB.

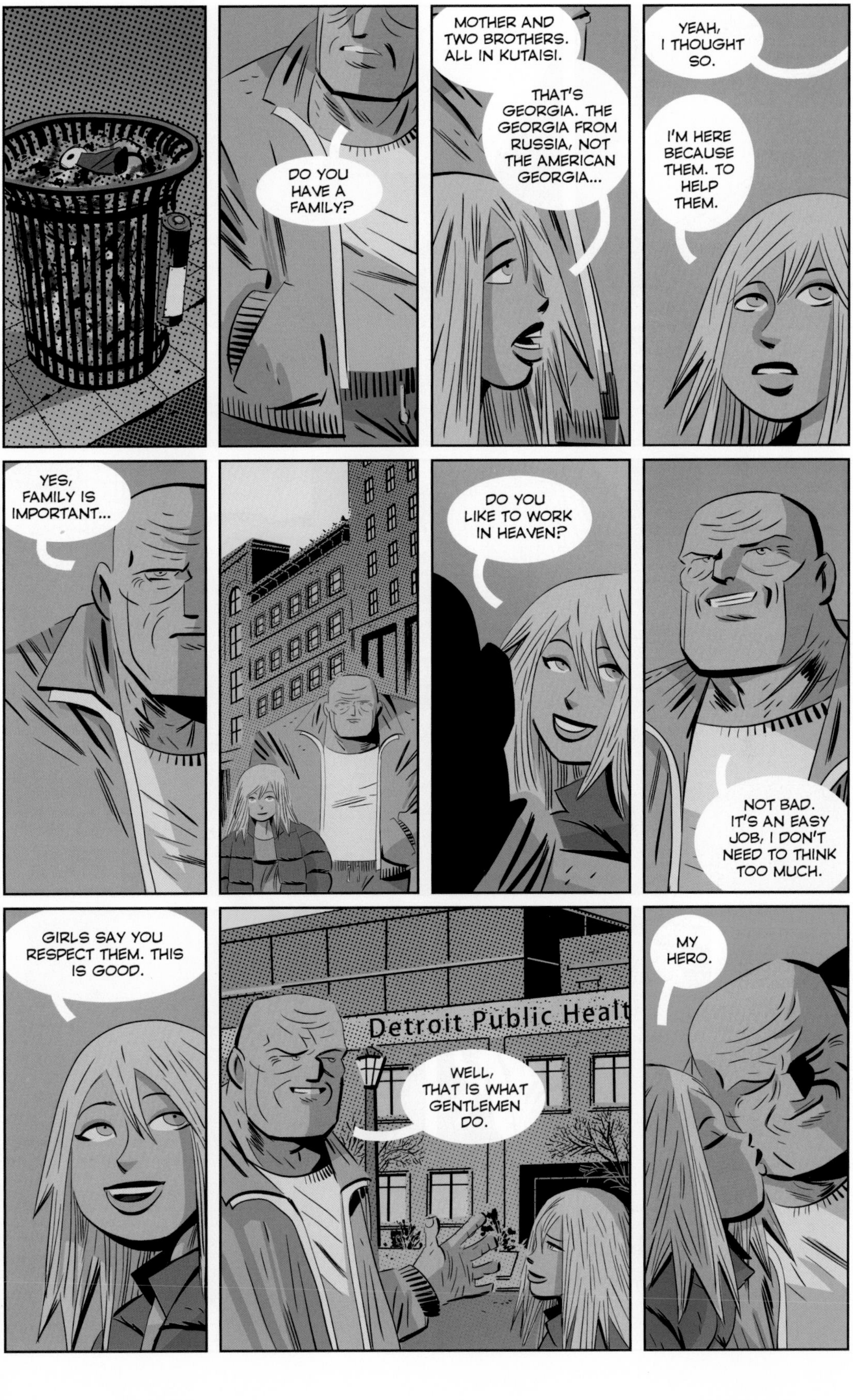
DO YOU HAVE A FAMILY?
MOTHER AND TWO BROTHERS. ALL IN KUTAISI.
THAT'S GEORGIA. THE GEORGIA FROM RUSSIA, NOT THE AMERICAN GEORGIA...
YEAH, I THOUGHT SO.
I'M HERE BECAUSE THEM. TO HELP THEM.
YES, FAMILY IS IMPORTANT...
DO YOU LIKE TO WORK IN HEAVEN?
NOT BAD. IT'S AN EASY JOB, I DON'T NEED TO THINK TOO MUCH.
GIRLS SAY YOU RESPECT THEM. THIS IS GOOD.
Detroit Public Healt
WELL, THAT IS WHAT GENTLEMEN DO.
MY HERO.

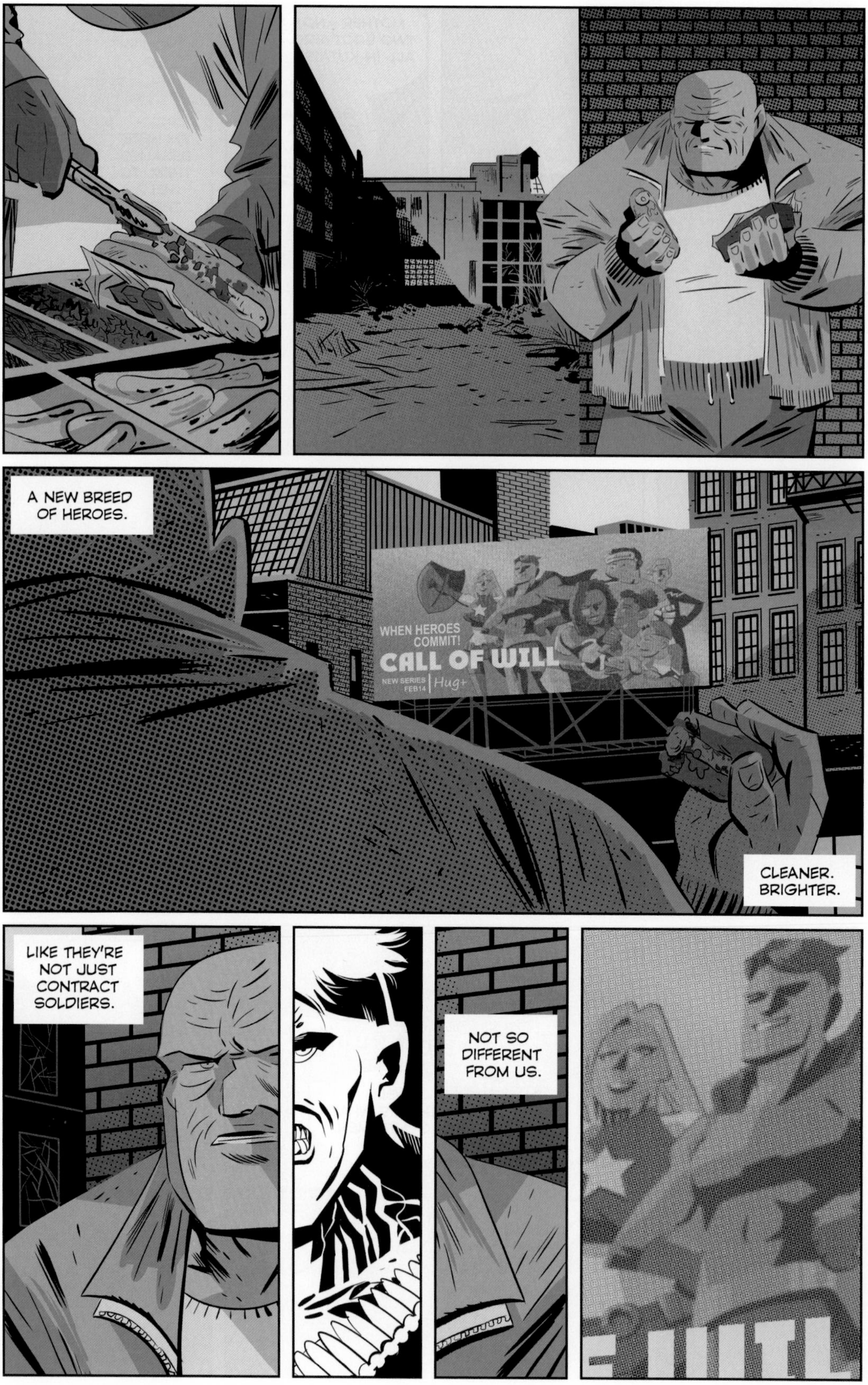
A NEW BREED OF HEROES.
WHEN HEROES COMMIT!
CALL OF WILL
NEW SERIES FEB14
Hug+
CLEANER. BRIGHTER.
LIKE THEY'RE NOT JUST CONTRACT SOLDIERS.
NOT SO DIFFERENT FROM US.

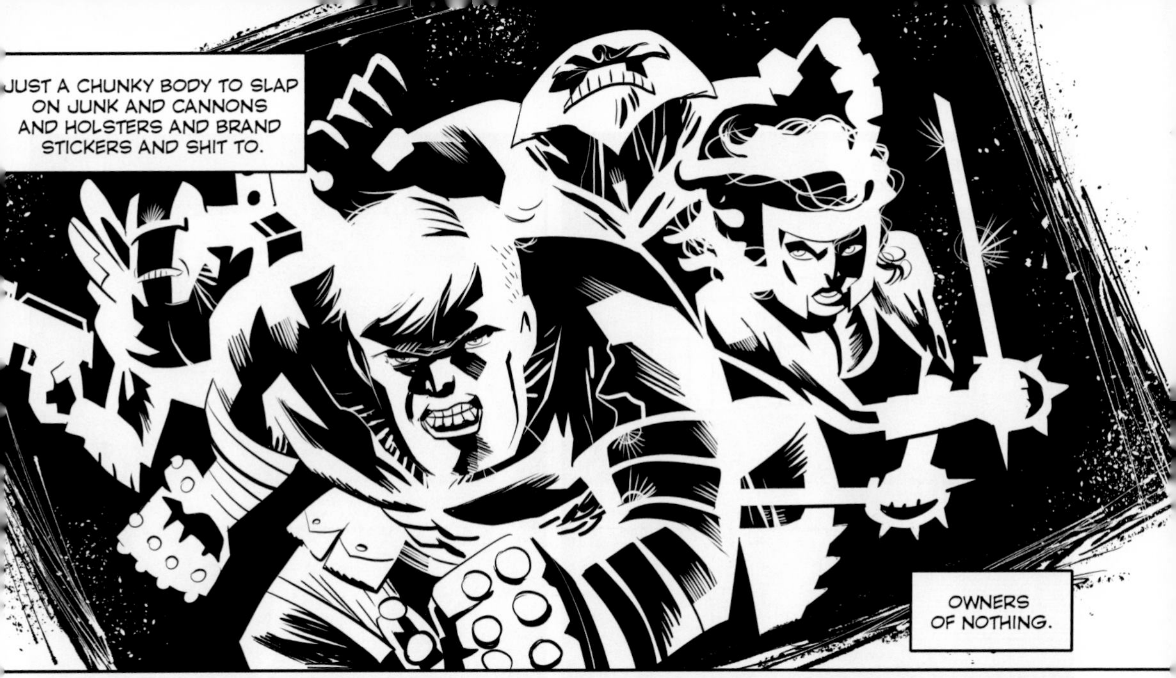
JUST A CHUNKY BODY TO SLAP ON JUNK AND CANNONS AND HOLSTERS AND BRAND STICKERS AND SHIT TO.
OWNERS OF NOTHING.

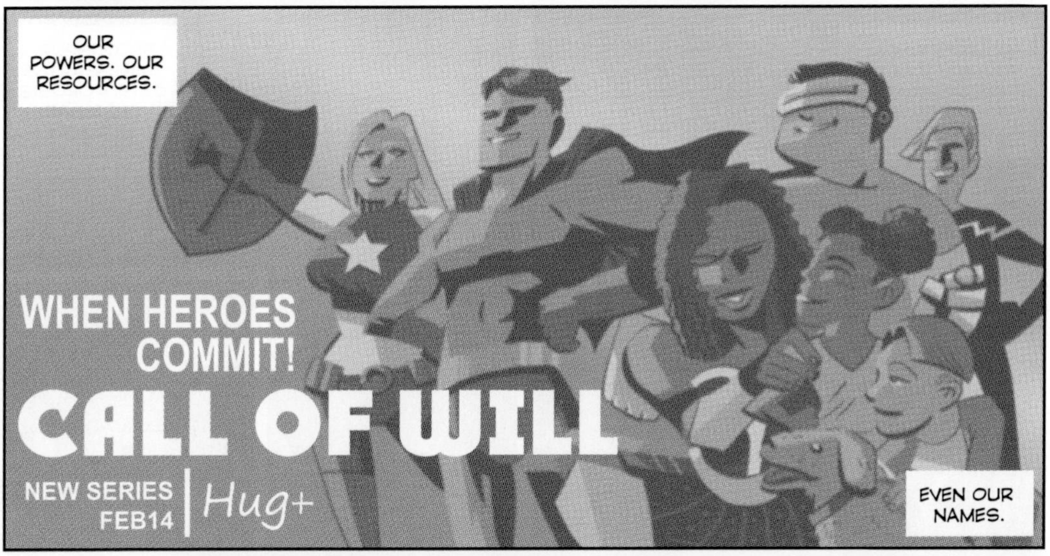
OUR POWERS. OUR RESOURCES.
WHEN HEROES COMMIT!
CALL OF WILL
NEW SERIES FEB14
Hug+
EVEN OUR NAMES.

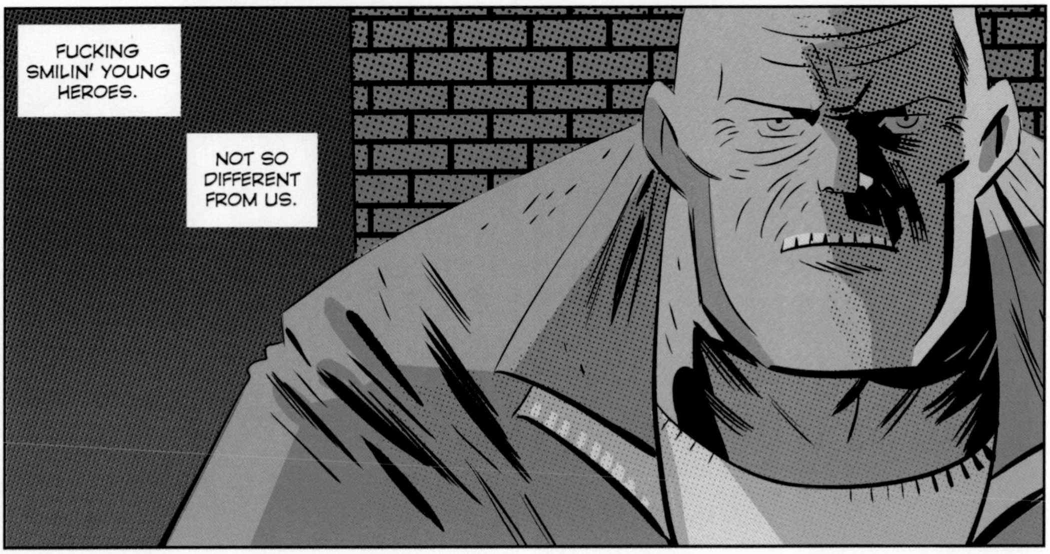
FUCKING SMILIN' YOUNG HEROES.
NOT SO DIFFERENT FROM US.

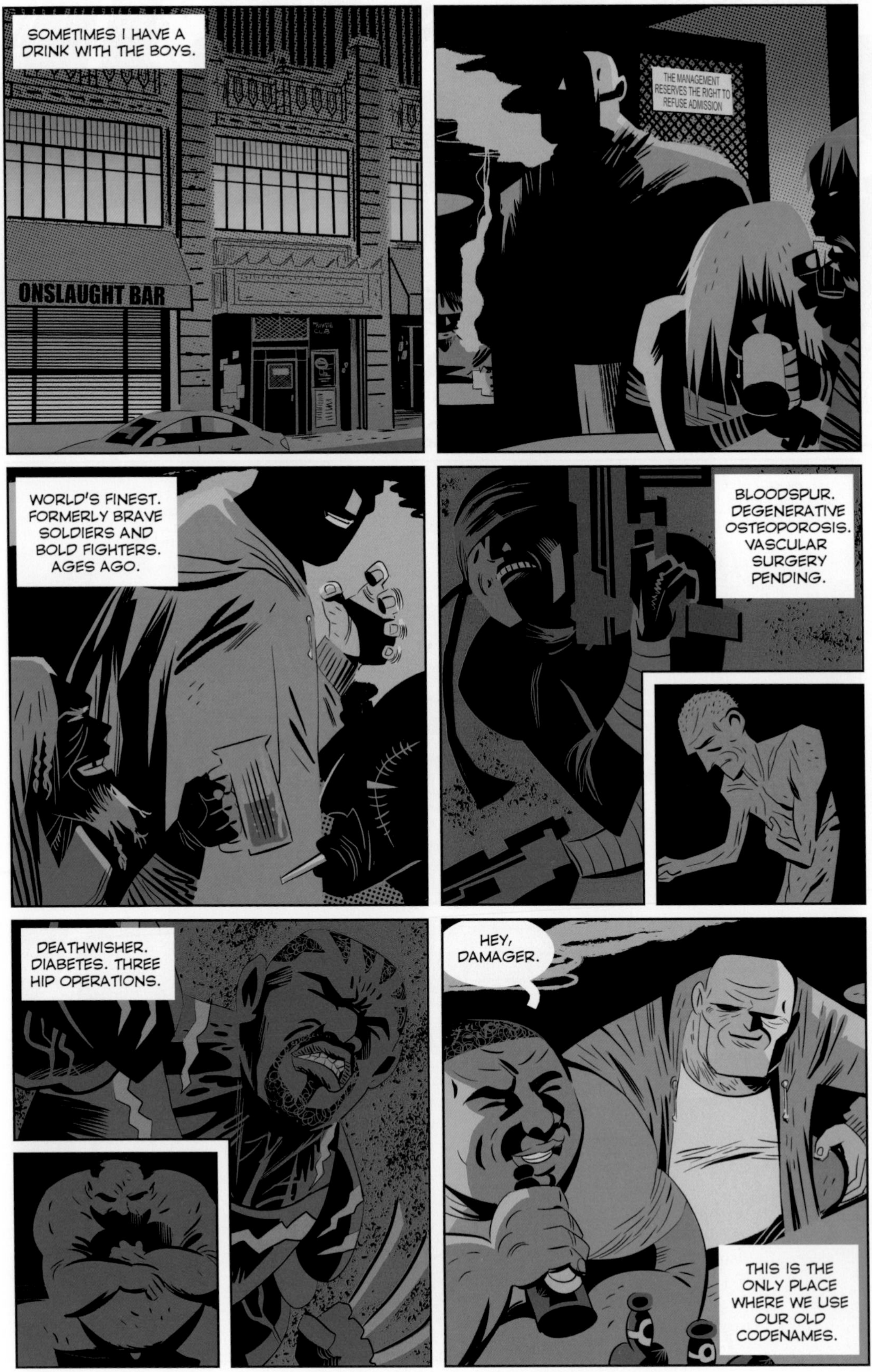
SOMETIMES I HAVE A DRINK WITH THE BOYS.
ONSLAUGHT BAR
THE MANAGEMENT RESERVES THE RIGHT TO REFUSE ADMISSION
WORLD'S FINEST. FORMERLY BRAVE SOLDIERS AND BOLD FIGHTERS. AGES AGO.
BLOODSPUR. DEGENERATIVE OSTEOPOROSIS. VASCULAR SURGERY PENDING.
DEATHWISHER. DIABETES. THREE HIP OPERATIONS.
HEY, DAMAGER.
THIS IS THE ONLY PLACE WHERE WE USE OUR OLD CODENAMES.

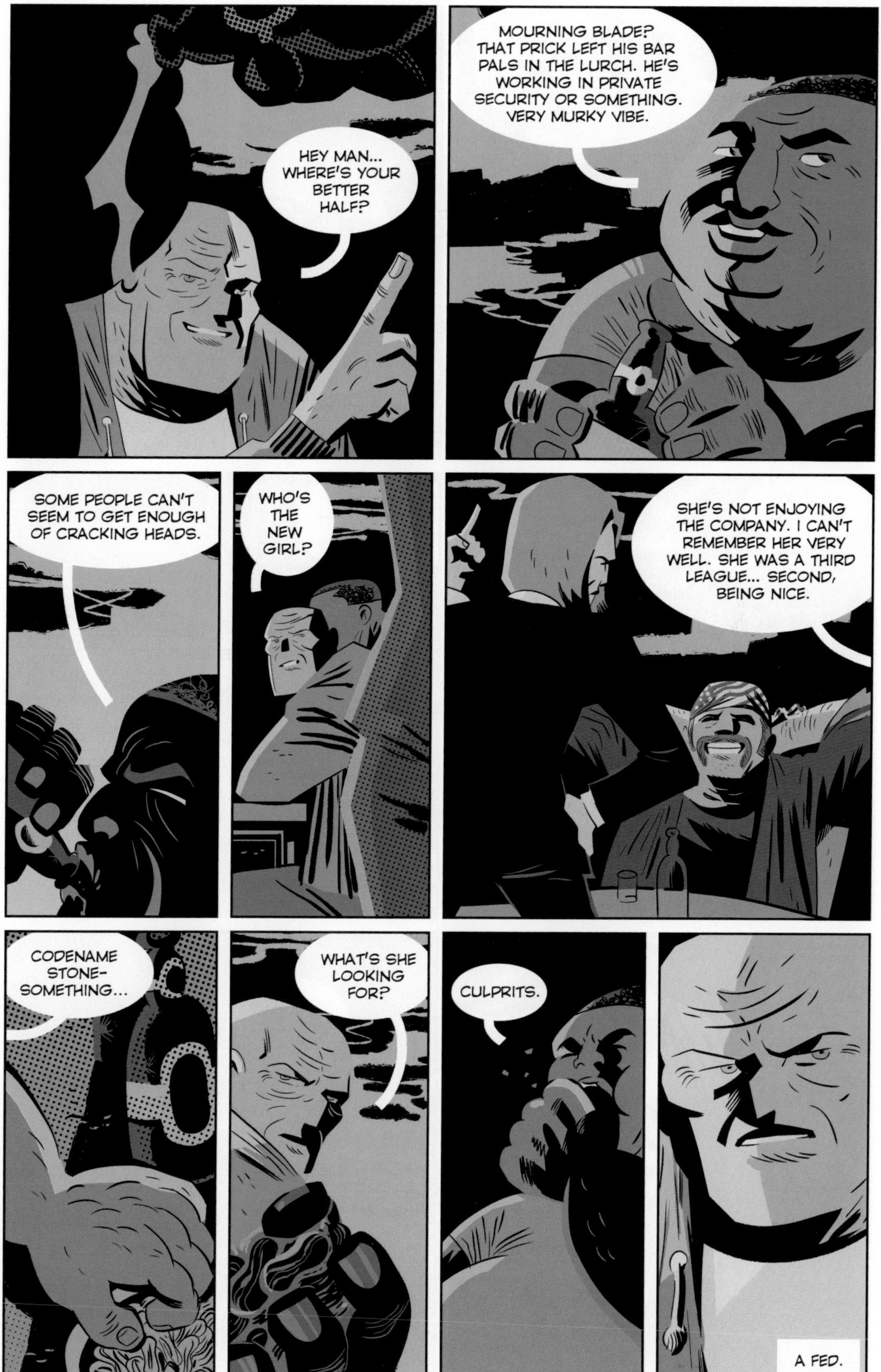
HEY MAN... WHERE'S YOUR BETTER HALF?
MOURNING BLADE? THAT PRICK LEFT HIS BAR PALS IN THE LURCH. HE'S WORKING IN PRIVATE SECURITY OR SOMETHING. VERY MURKY VIBE.
SOME PEOPLE CAN'T SEEM TO GET ENOUGH OF CRACKING HEADS.
WHO'S THE NEW GIRL?
SHE'S NOT ENJOYING THE COMPANY. I CAN'T REMEMBER HER VERY WELL. SHE WAS A THIRD LEAGUE... SECOND, BEING NICE.
CODENAME STONE-SOMETHING...
WHAT'S SHE LOOKING FOR?
CULPRITS.
A FED.

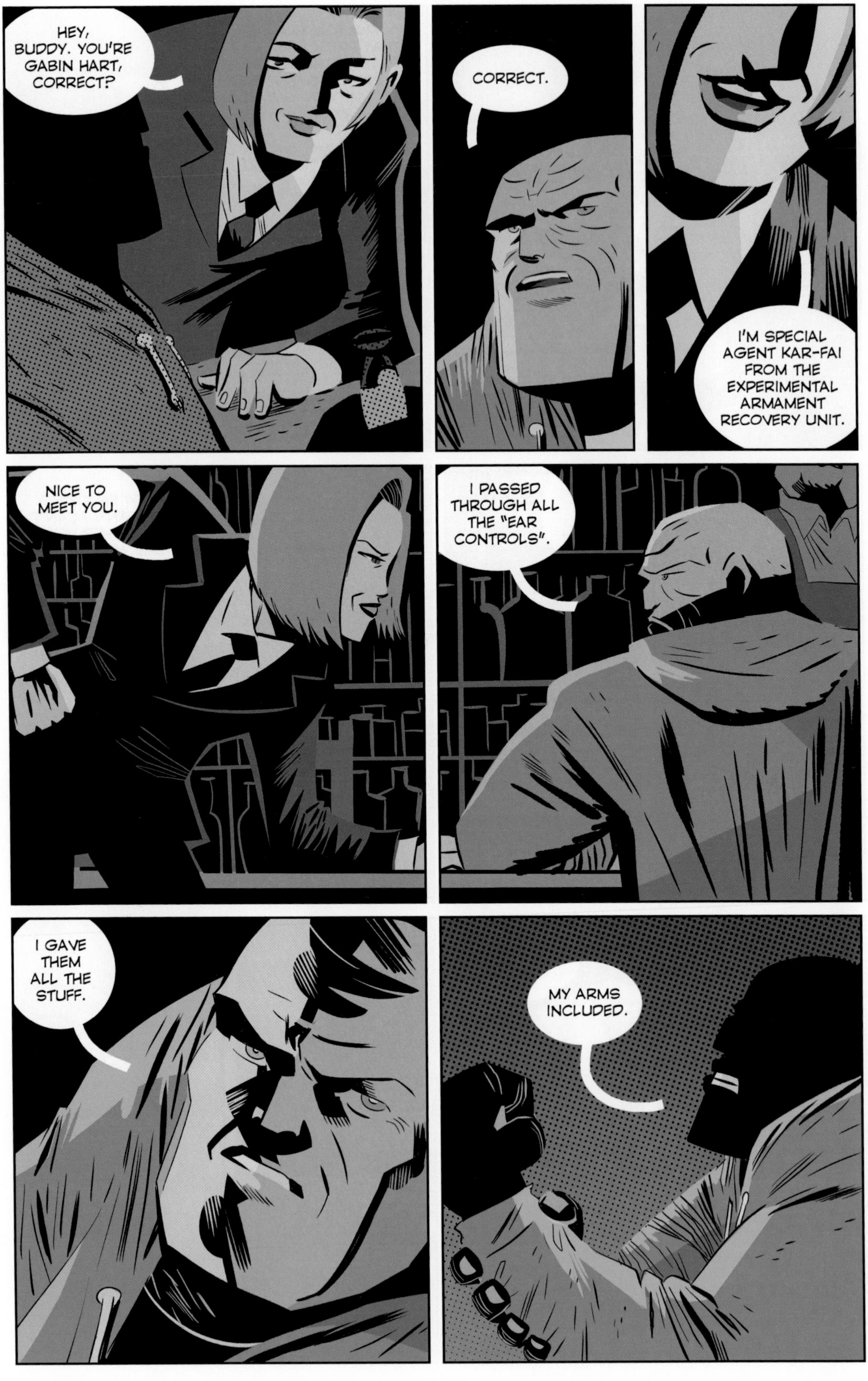
HEY, BUDDY. YOU'RE GABIN HART, CORRECT?
CORRECT.
I'M SPECIAL AGENT KAR-FAI FROM THE EXPERIMENTAL ARMAMENT RECOVERY UNIT.
NICE TO MEET YOU.
I PASSED THROUGH ALL THE "EAR CONTROLS".
I GAVE THEM ALL THE STUFF.
MY ARMS INCLUDED.

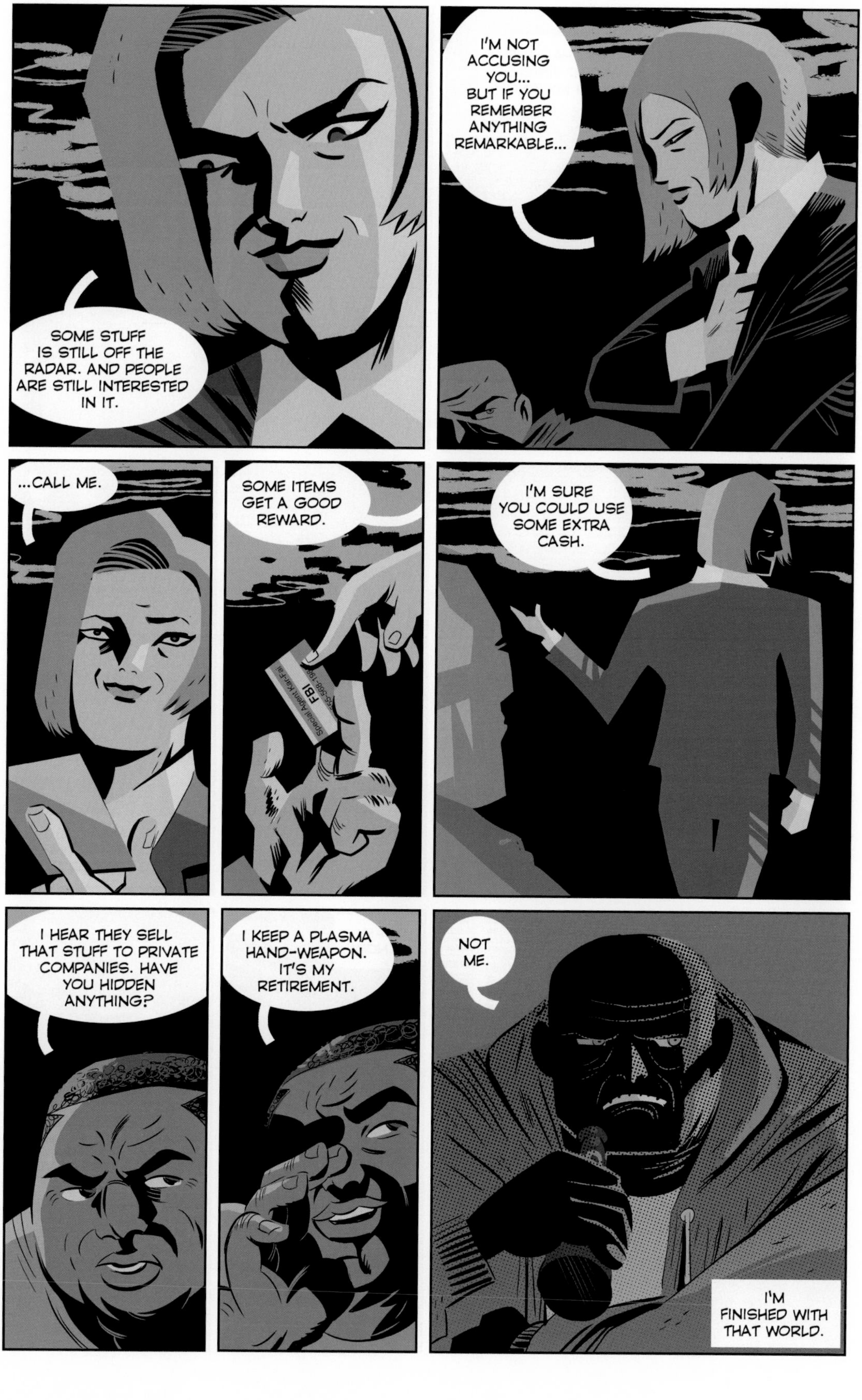
SOME STUFF IS STILL OFF THE RADAR. AND PEOPLE ARE STILL INTERESTED IN IT.
I'M NOT ACCUSING YOU... BUT IF YOU REMEMBER ANYTHING REMARKABLE...
...CALL ME.
SOME ITEMS GET A GOOD REWARD.
FBI
I'M SURE YOU COULD USE SOME EXTRA CASH.
I HEAR THEY SELL THAT STUFF TO PRIVATE COMPANIES. HAVE YOU HIDDEN ANYTHING?
I KEEP A PLASMA HAND-WEAPON. IT'S MY RETIREMENT.
NOT ME.
I'M FINISHED WITH THAT WORLD.

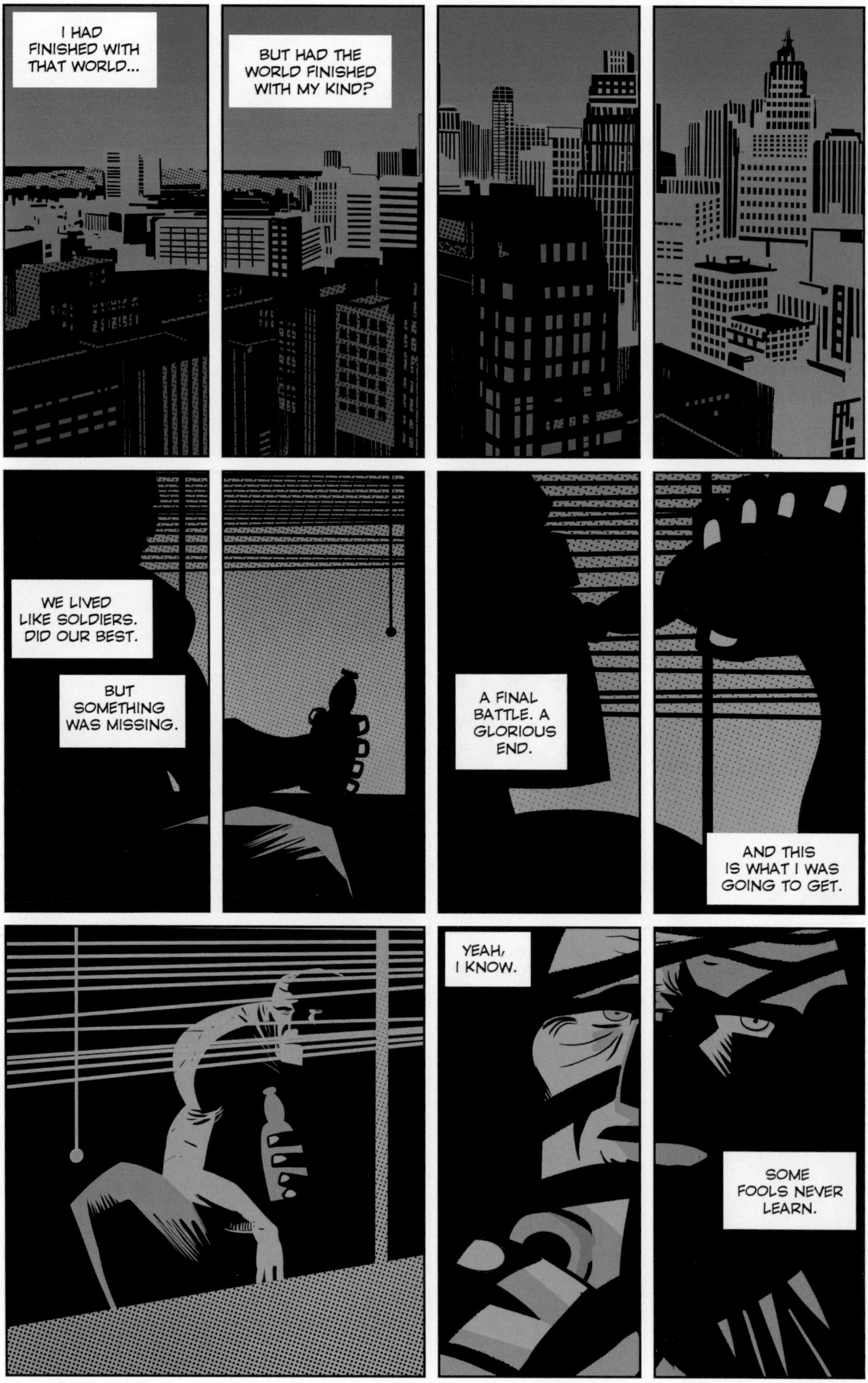
I HAD FINISHED WITH THAT WORLD...
BUT HAD THE WORLD FINISHED WITH MY KIND?
WE LIVED LIKE SOLDIERS. DID OUR BEST.
BUT SOMETHING WAS MISSING.
A FINAL BATTLE. A GLORIOUS END.
AND THIS IS WHAT I WAS GOING TO GET.
YEAH, I KNOW.
SOME FOOLS NEVER LEARN.

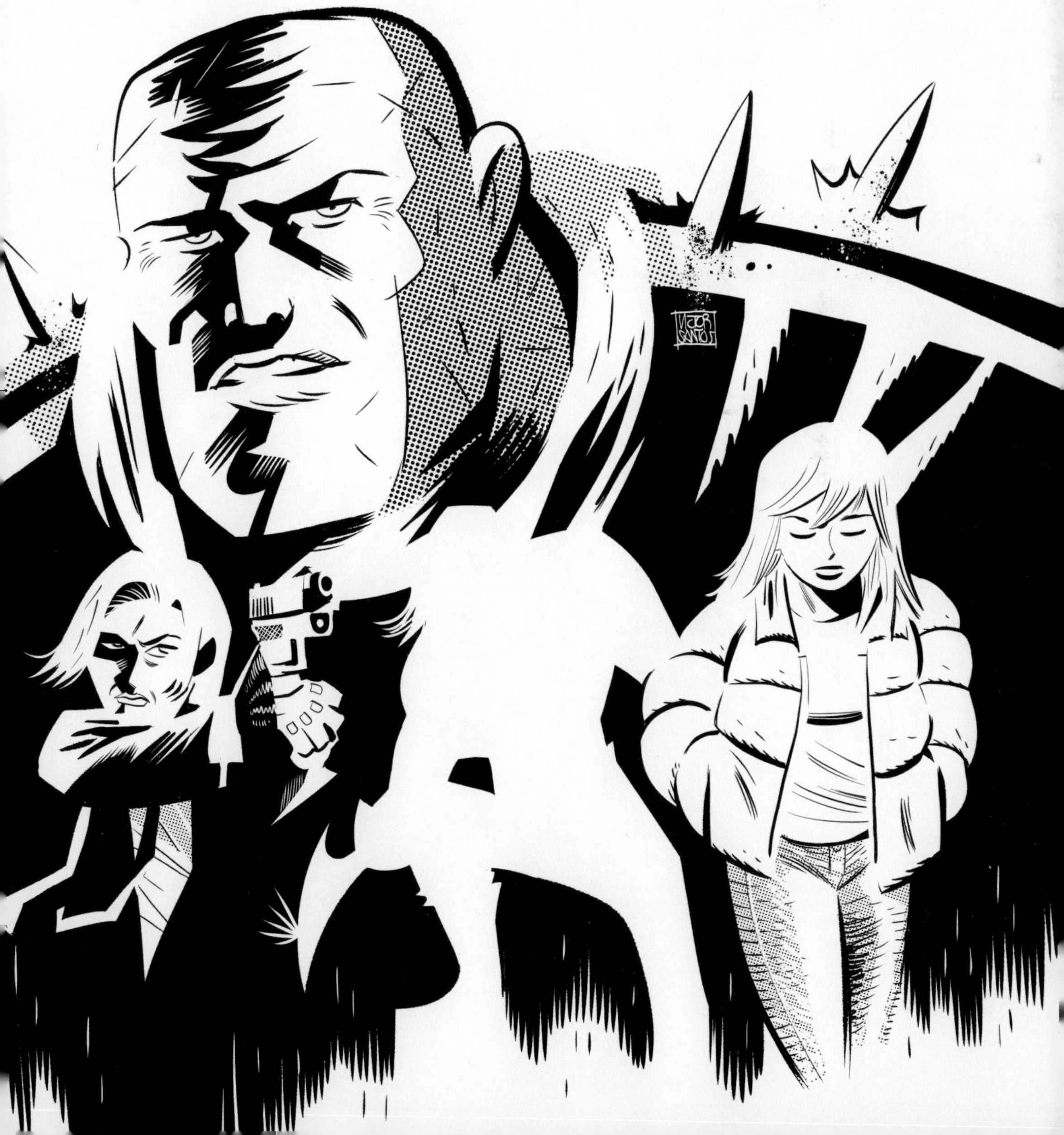

# VICTOR SANTOS
# UNTIL MY KNUCKLES
# BLEED
## EXTREMELY DAMAGED
### PART 2

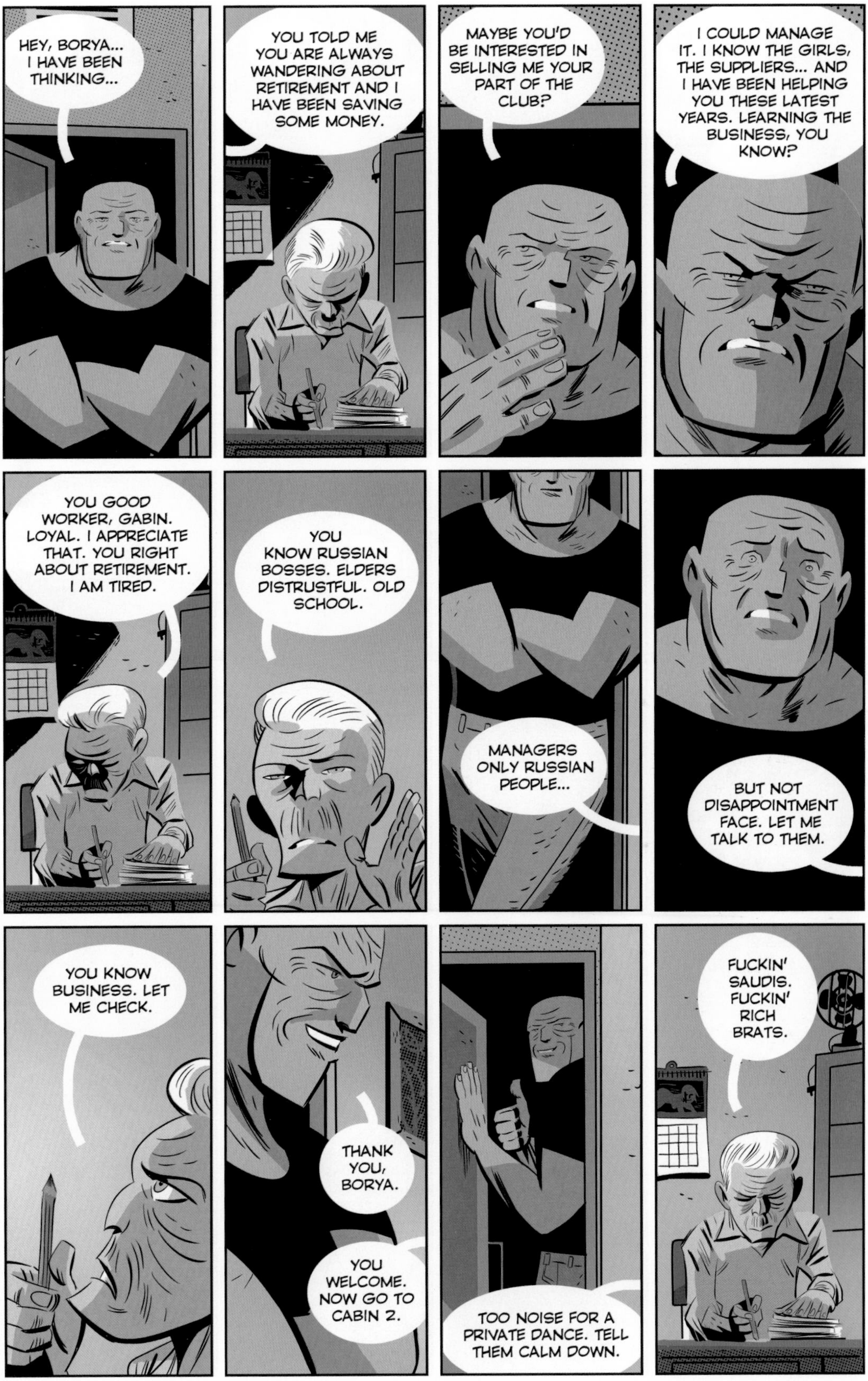
HEY, BORYA... I HAVE BEEN THINKING...
YOU TOLD ME YOU ARE ALWAYS WANDERING ABOUT RETIREMENT AND I HAVE BEEN SAVING SOME MONEY.
MAYBE YOU'D BE INTERESTED IN SELLING ME YOUR PART OF THE CLUB?
I COULD MANAGE IT. I KNOW THE GIRLS, THE SUPPLIERS... AND I HAVE BEEN HELPING YOU THESE LATEST YEARS. LEARNING THE BUSINESS, YOU KNOW?
YOU GOOD WORKER, GABIN. LOYAL. I APPRECIATE THAT. YOU RIGHT ABOUT RETIREMENT. I AM TIRED.
YOU KNOW RUSSIAN BOSSES. ELDERS DISTRUSTFUL. OLD SCHOOL.
MANAGERS ONLY RUSSIAN PEOPLE...
BUT NOT DISAPPOINTMENT FACE. LET ME TALK TO THEM.
YOU KNOW BUSINESS. LET ME CHECK.
THANK YOU, BORYA.
YOU WELCOME. NOW GO TO CABIN 2.
TOO NOISE FOR A PRIVATE DANCE. TELL THEM CALM DOWN.
FUCKIN' SAUDIS. FUCKIN' RICH BRATS.

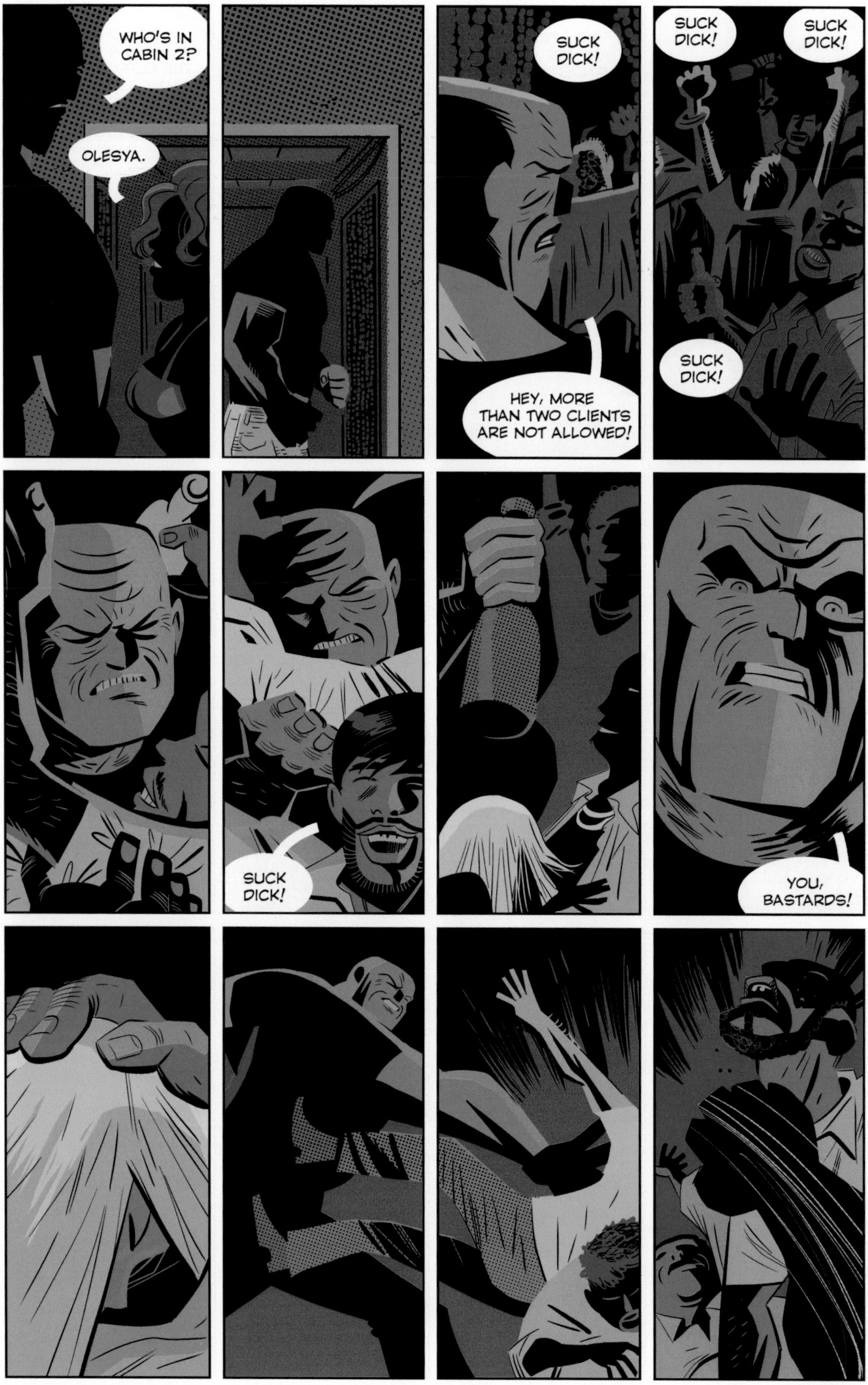
WHO'S IN CABIN 2?
OLESYA.
SUCK DICK!
HEY, MORE THAN TWO CLIENTS ARE NOT ALLOWED!
SUCK DICK!
SUCK DICK!
SUCK DICK!
SUCK DICK!
YOU, BASTARDS!

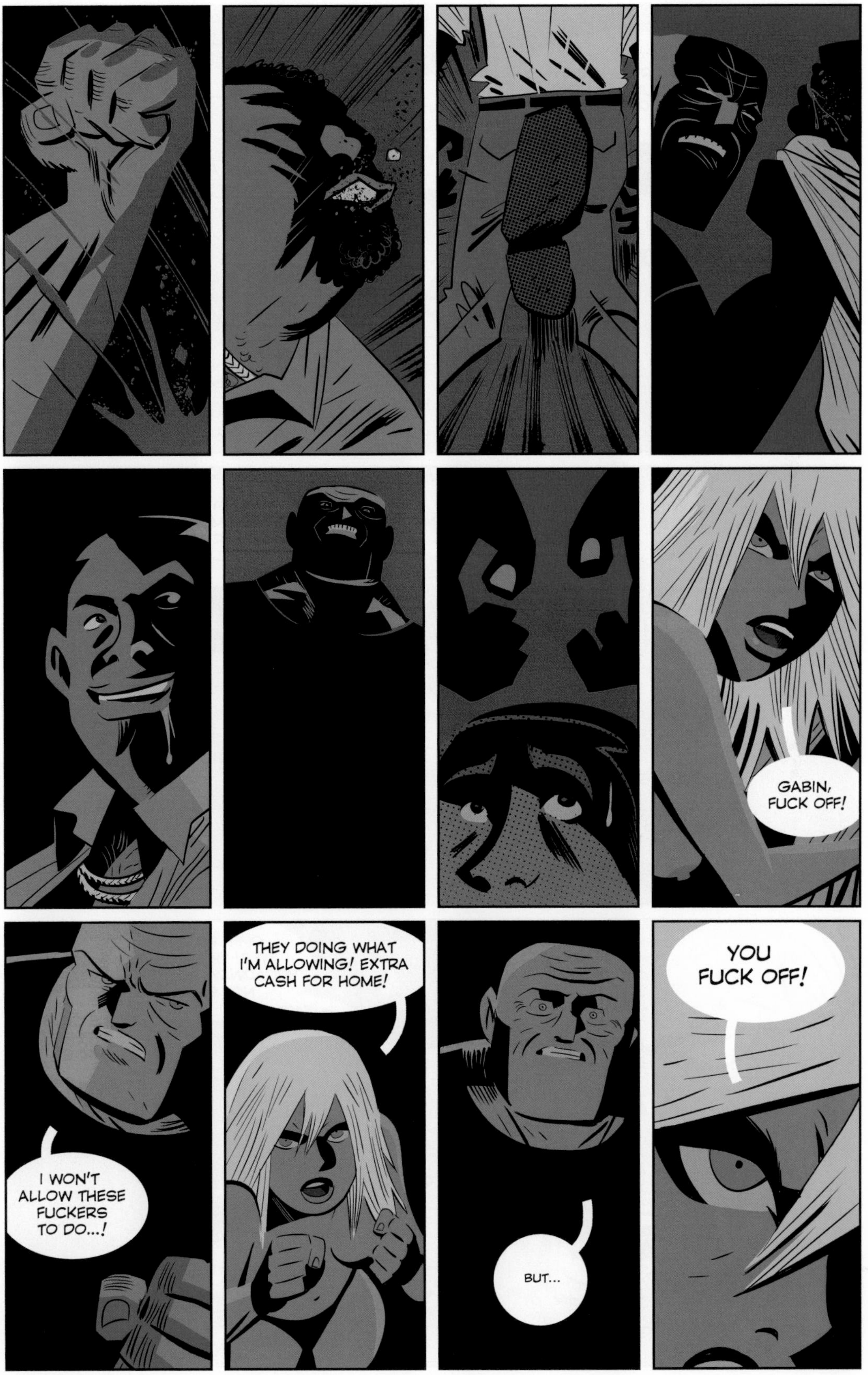
GABIN,
FUCK OFF!
I WON'T
ALLOW THESE
FUCKERS
TO DO...!
THEY DOING WHAT
I'M ALLOWING! EXTRA
CASH FOR HOME!
BUT...
YOU
FUCK OFF!

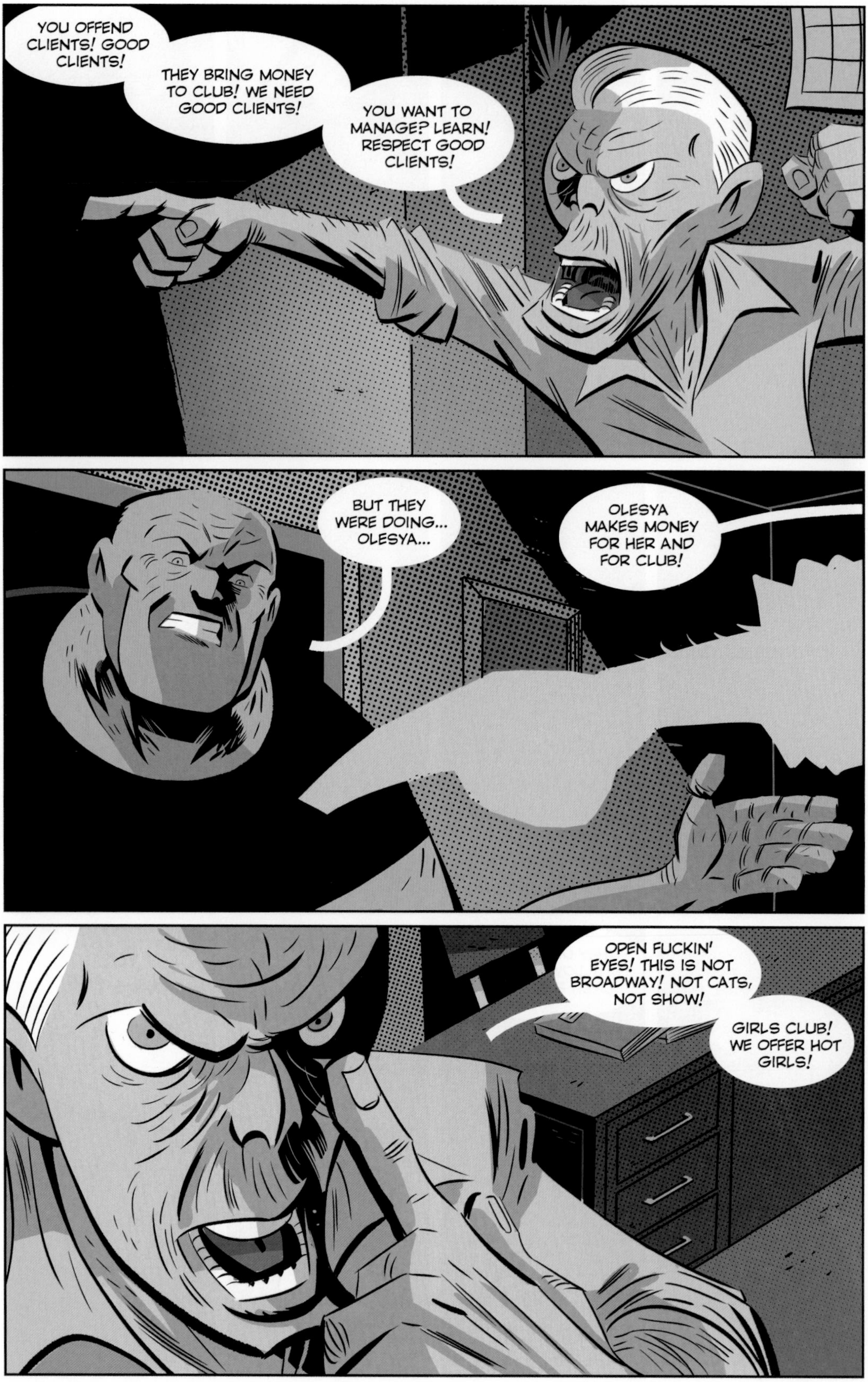

YOU OFFEND CLIENTS! GOOD CLIENTS!
THEY BRING MONEY TO CLUB! WE NEED GOOD CLIENTS!
YOU WANT TO MANAGE? LEARN! RESPECT GOOD CLIENTS!
BUT THEY WERE DOING... OLESYA...
OLESYA MAKES MONEY FOR HER AND FOR CLUB!
OPEN FUCKIN' EYES! THIS IS NOT BROADWAY! NOT CATS, NOT SHOW!
GIRLS CLUB! WE OFFER HOT GIRLS!

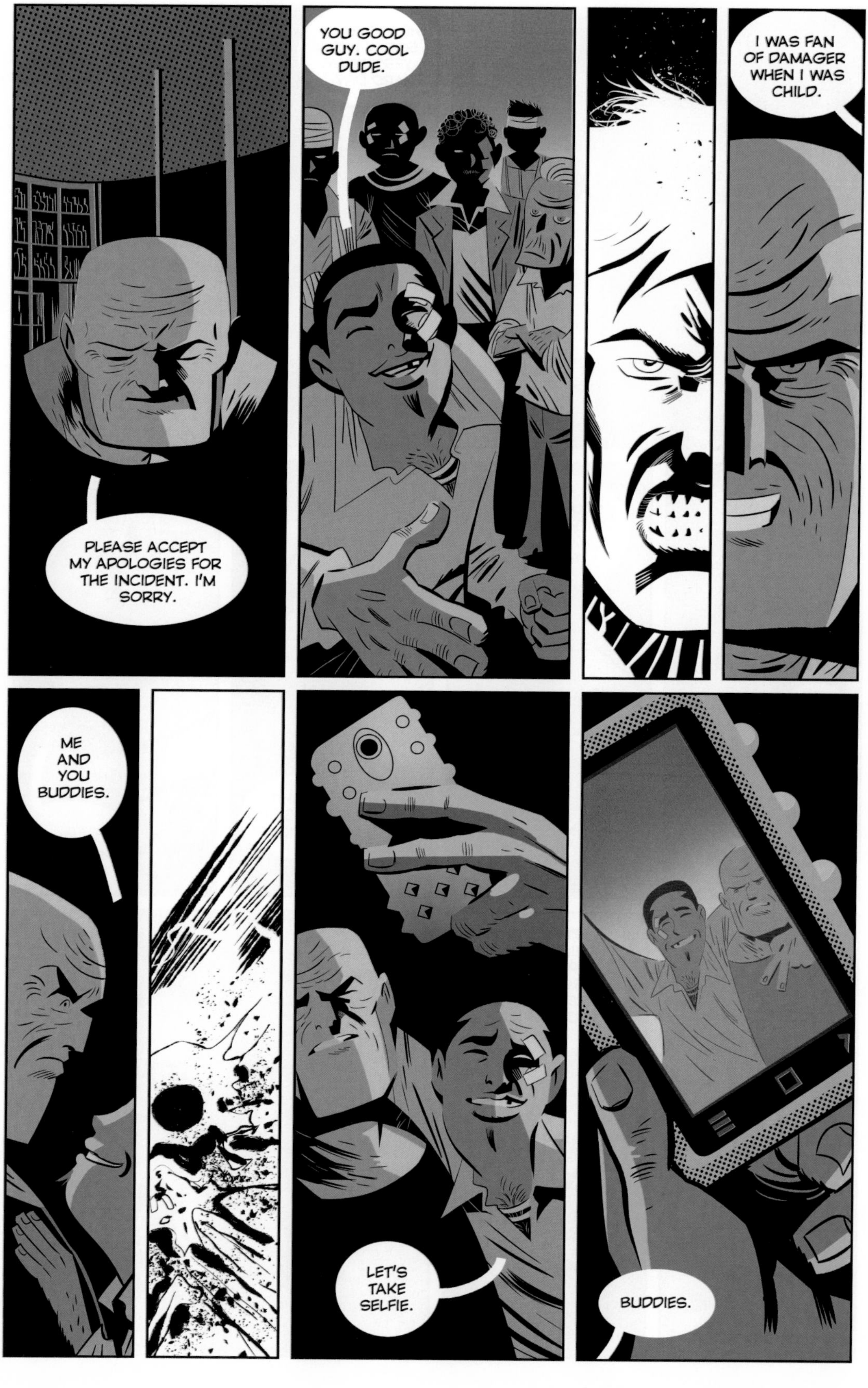
PLEASE ACCEPT MY APOLOGIES FOR THE INCIDENT. I'M SORRY.
YOU GOOD GUY. COOL DUDE.
I WAS FAN OF DAMAGER WHEN I WAS CHILD.
ME AND YOU BUDDIES.
LET'S TAKE SELFIE.
BUDDIES.

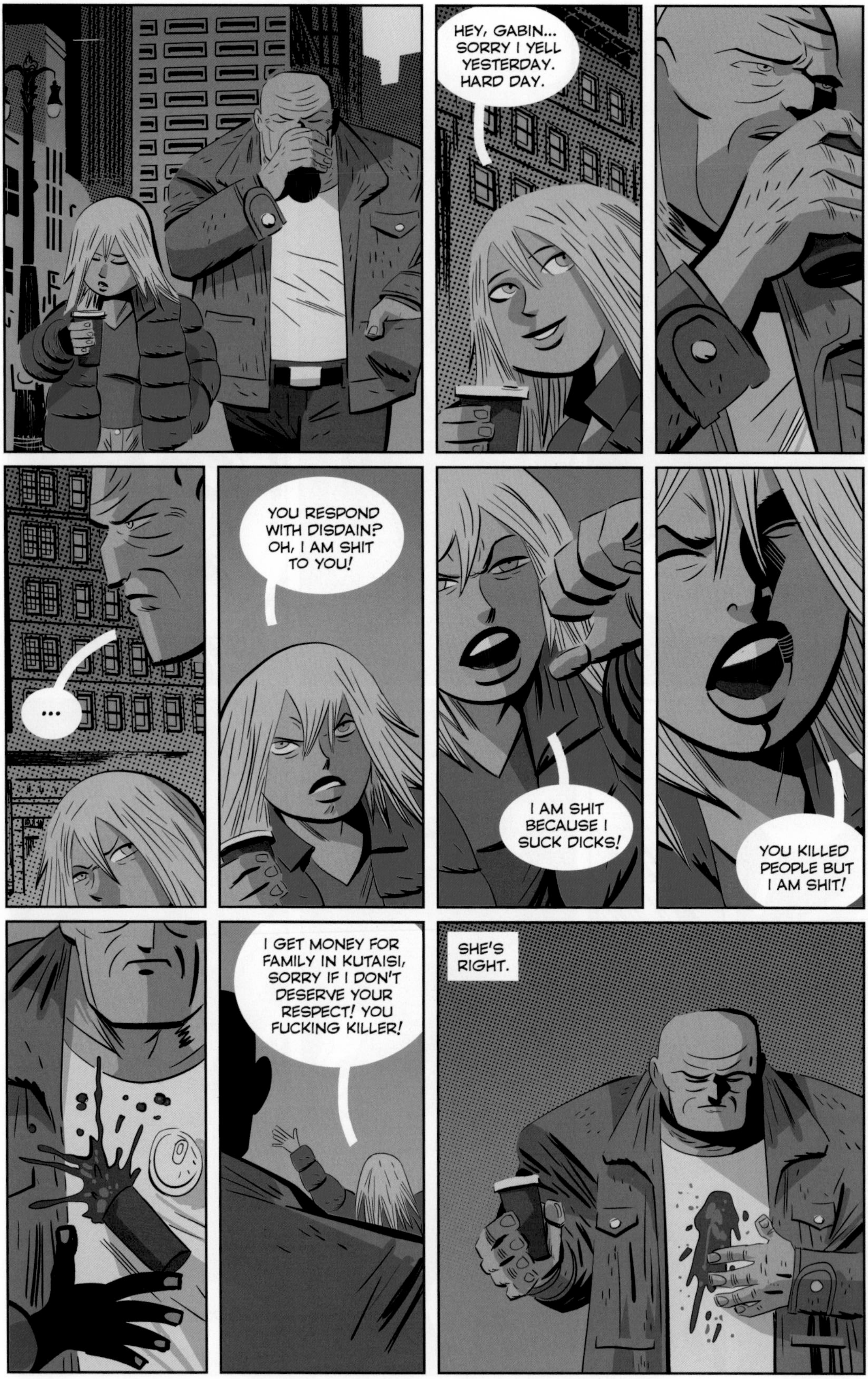
HEY, GABIN... SORRY I YELL YESTERDAY. HARD DAY.
...
YOU RESPOND WITH DISDAIN? OH, I AM SHIT TO YOU!
I AM SHIT BECAUSE I SUCK DICKS!
YOU KILLED PEOPLE BUT I AM SHIT!
I GET MONEY FOR FAMILY IN KUTAISI, SORRY IF I DON'T DESERVE YOUR RESPECT! YOU FUCKING KILLER!
SHE'S RIGHT.

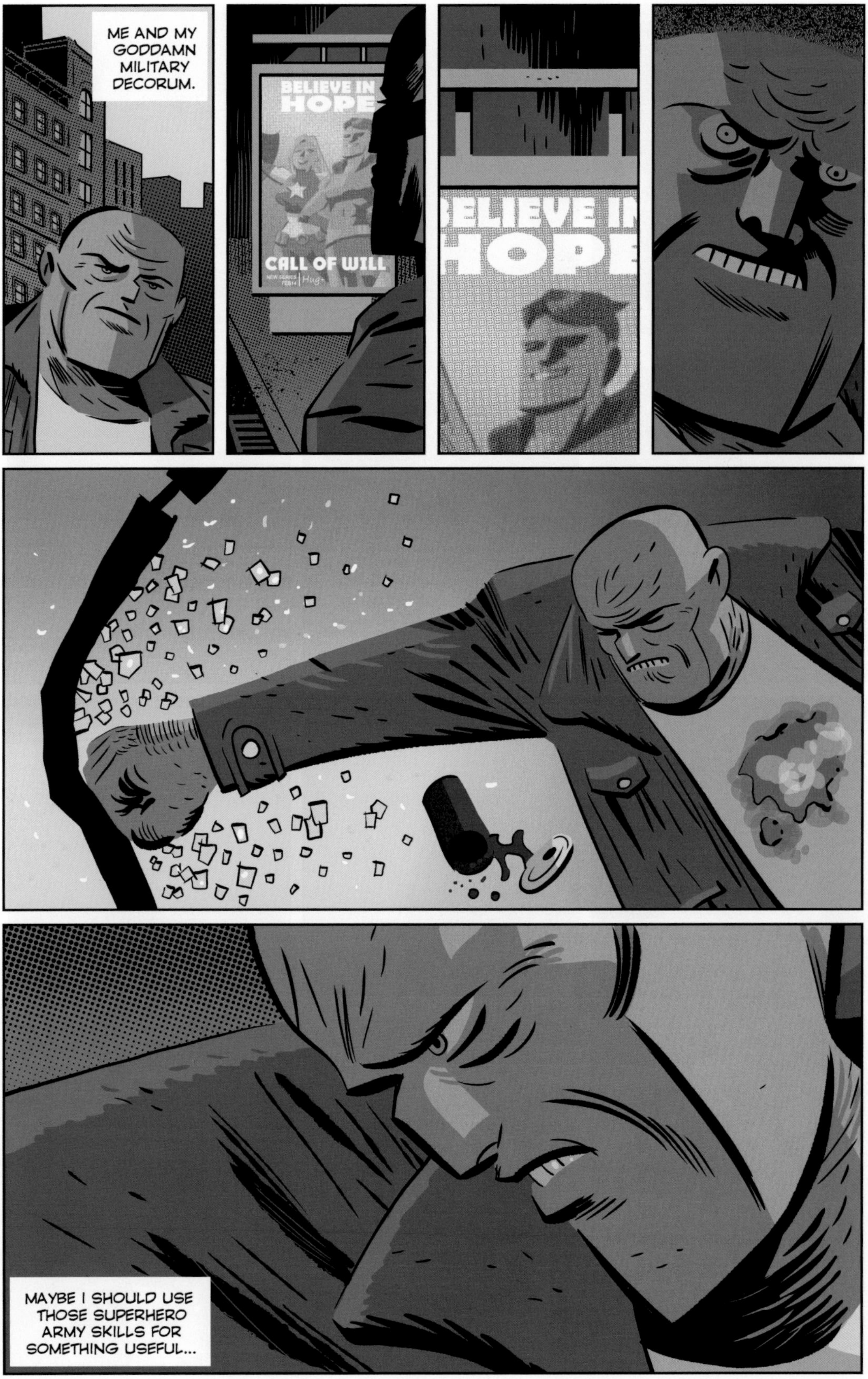
ME AND MY GODDAMN MILITARY DECORUM.
BELIEVE IN HOPE
CALL OF WILL
BELIEVE IN HOPE
MAYBE I SHOULD USE THOSE SUPERHERO ARMY SKILLS FOR SOMETHING USEFUL...

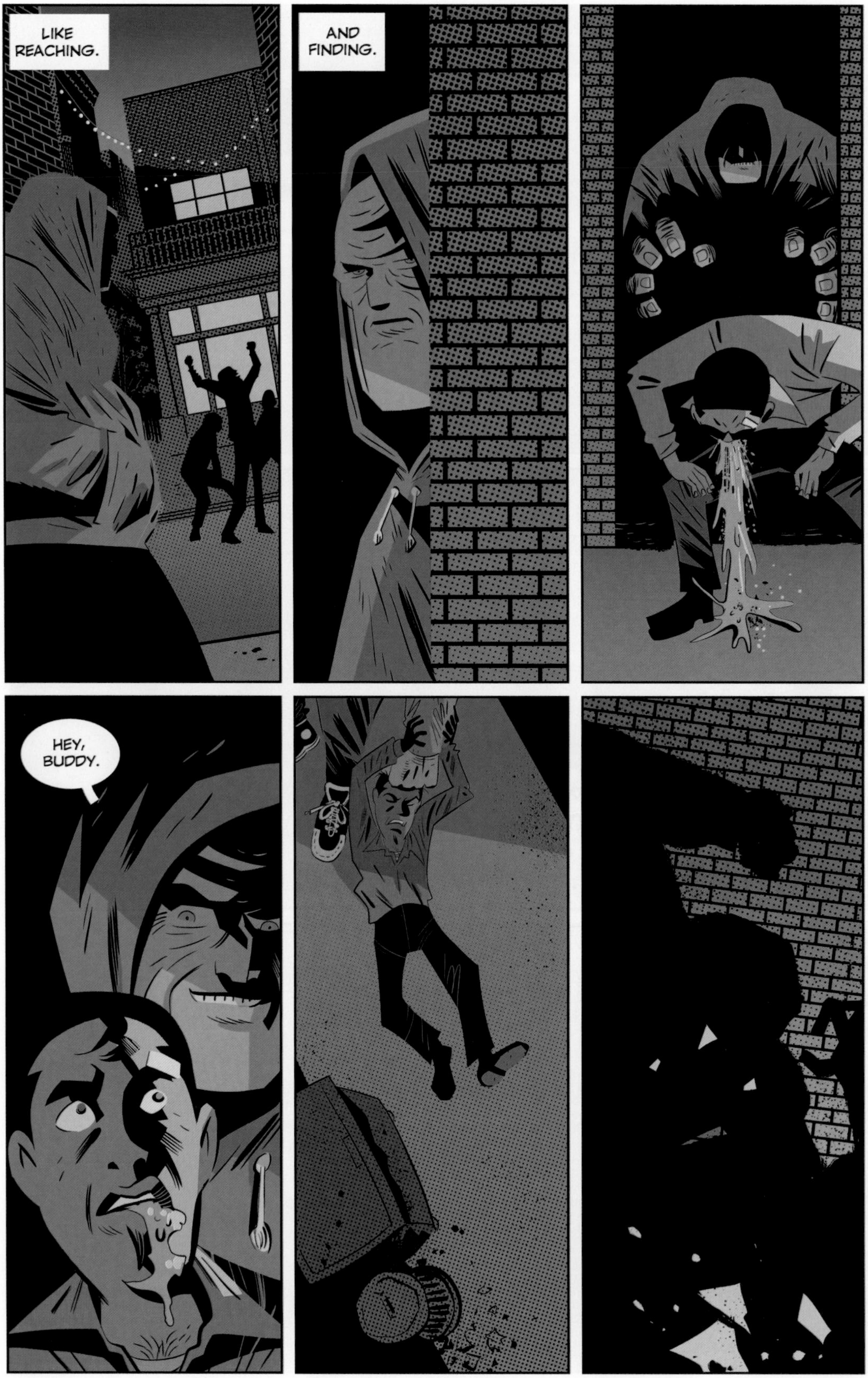
LIKE REACHING.
AND FINDING.
HEY, BUDDY.

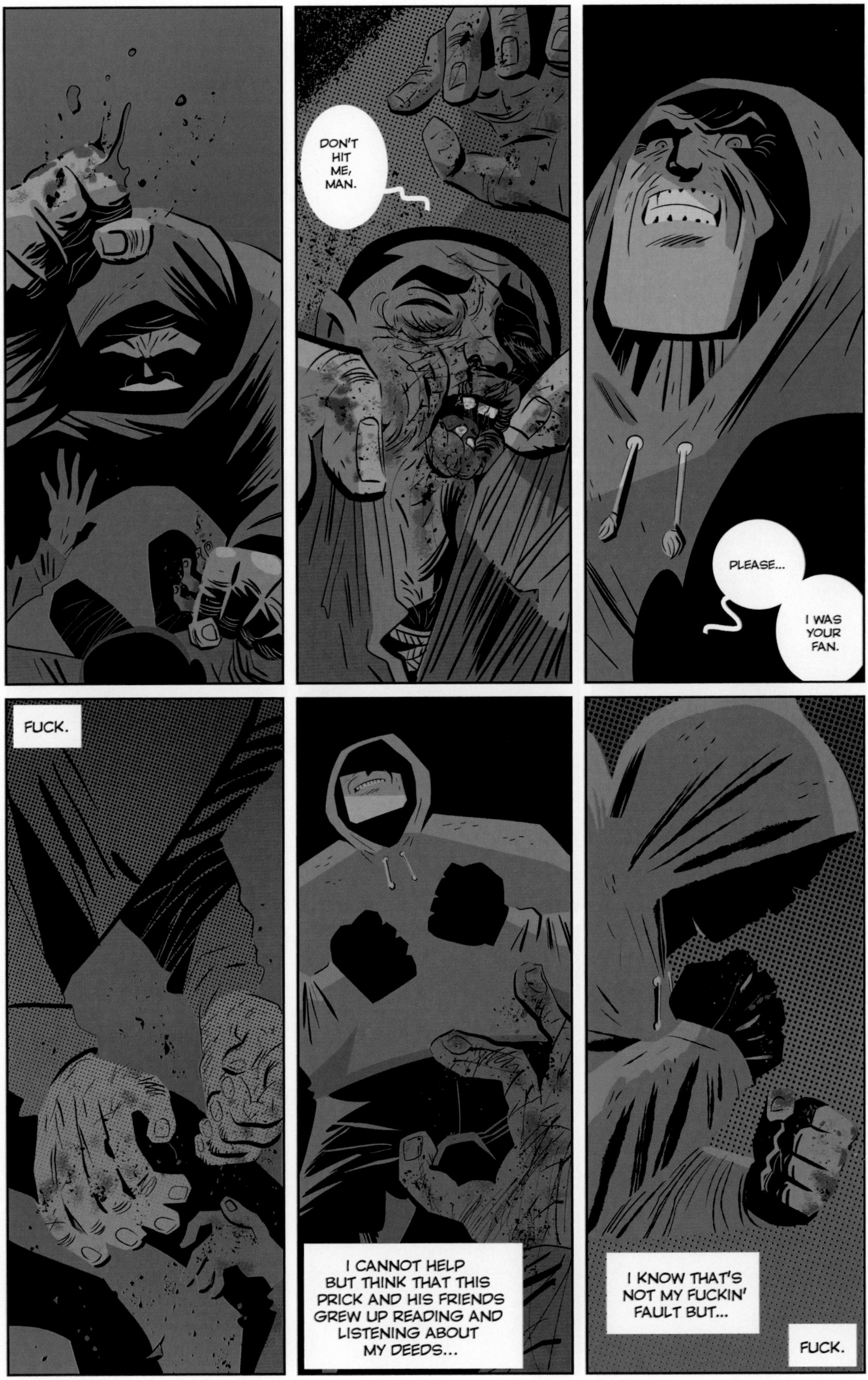

DON'T HIT ME, MAN.
PLEASE...
I WAS YOUR FAN.
FUCK.
I CANNOT HELP BUT THINK THAT THIS PRICK AND HIS FRIENDS GREW UP READING AND LISTENING ABOUT MY DEEDS...
I KNOW THAT'S NOT MY FUCKIN' FAULT BUT...
FUCK.

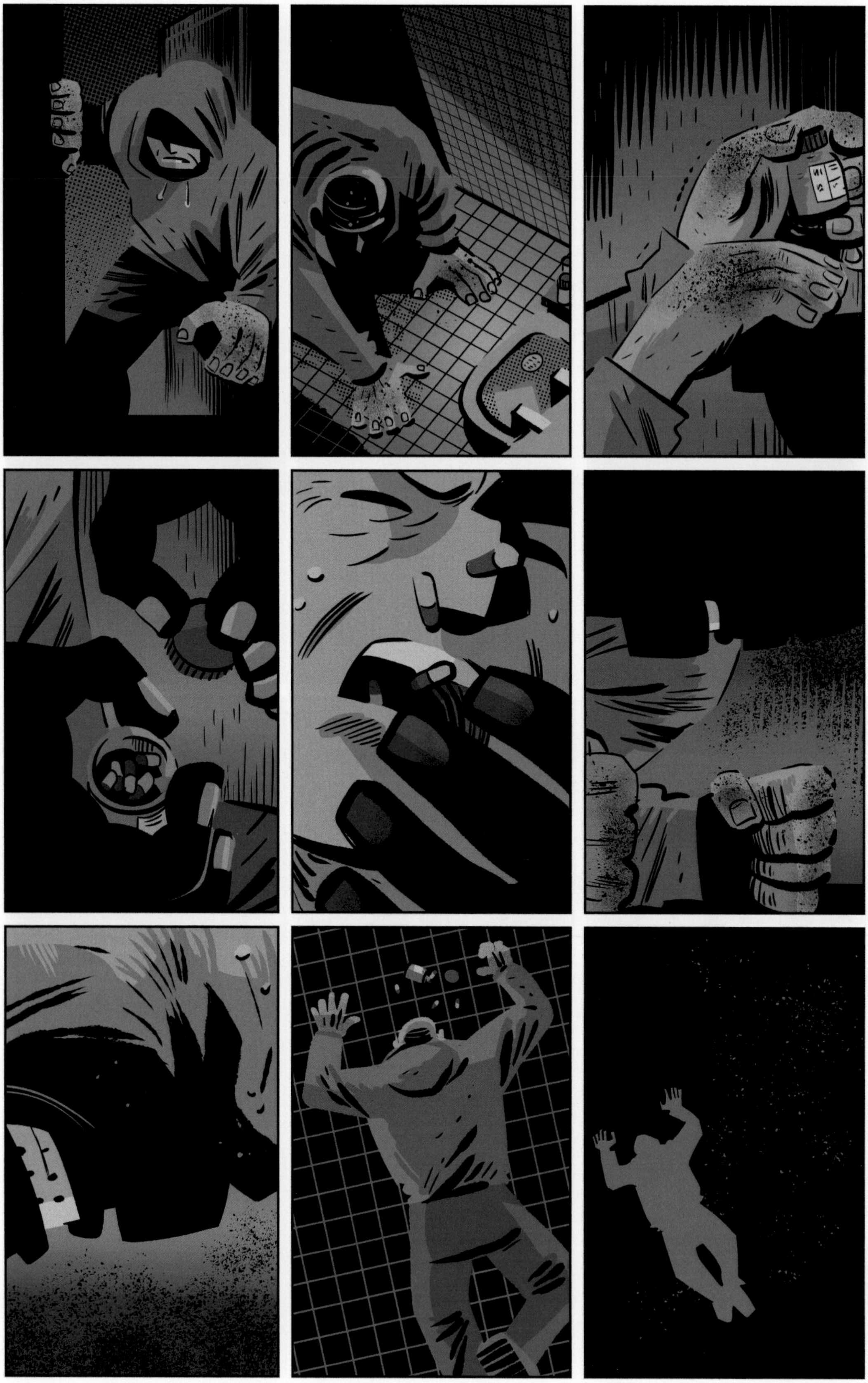

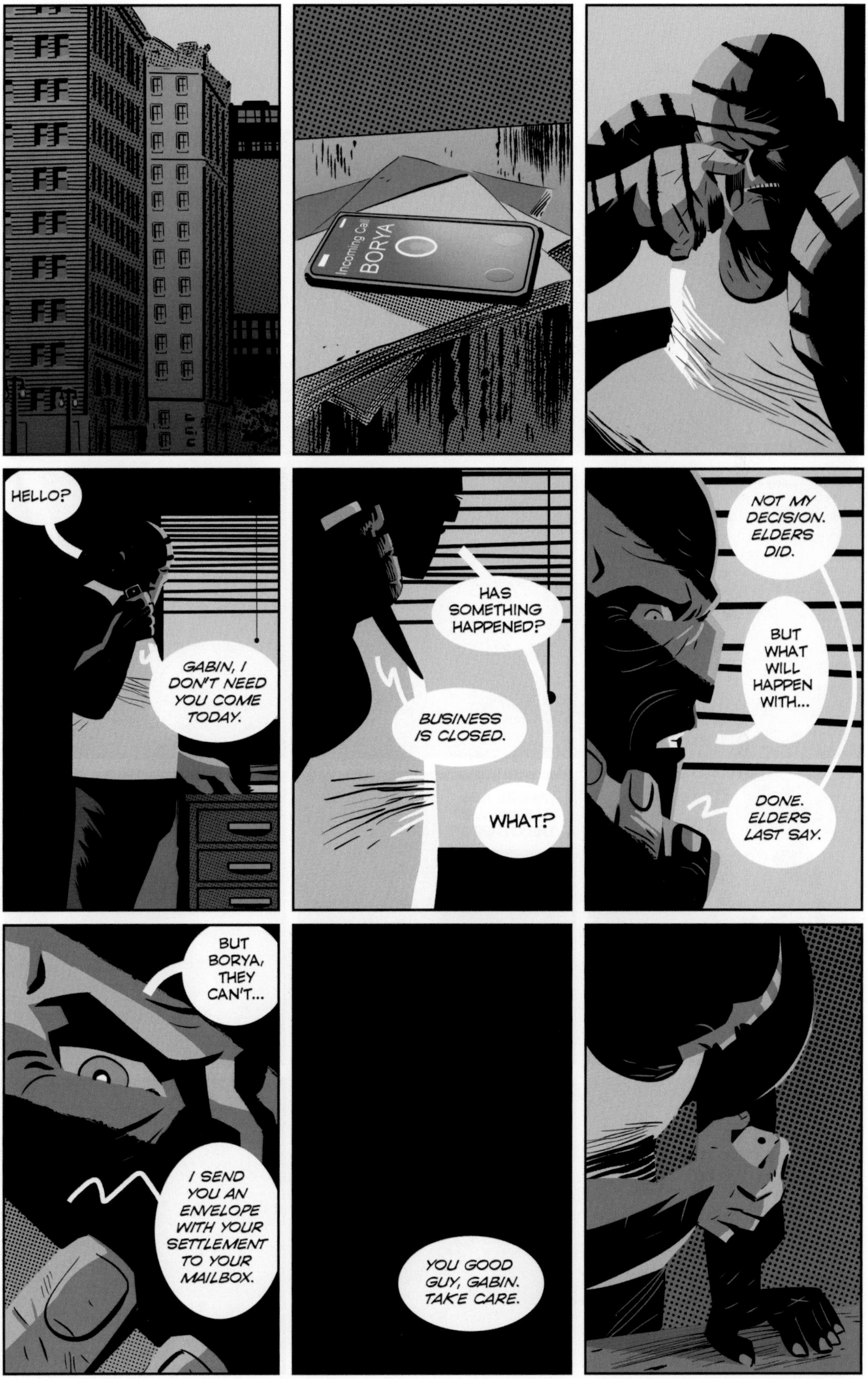
Incoming Call
BORYA
HELLO?
GABIN, I DON'T NEED YOU COME TODAY.
HAS SOMETHING HAPPENED?
BUSINESS IS CLOSED.
WHAT?
NOT MY DECISION. ELDERS DID.
BUT WHAT WILL HAPPEN WITH...
DONE. ELDERS LAST SAY.
BUT BORYA, THEY CAN'T...
I SEND YOU AN ENVELOPE WITH YOUR SETTLEMENT TO YOUR MAILBOX.
YOU GOOD GUY, GABIN. TAKE CARE.

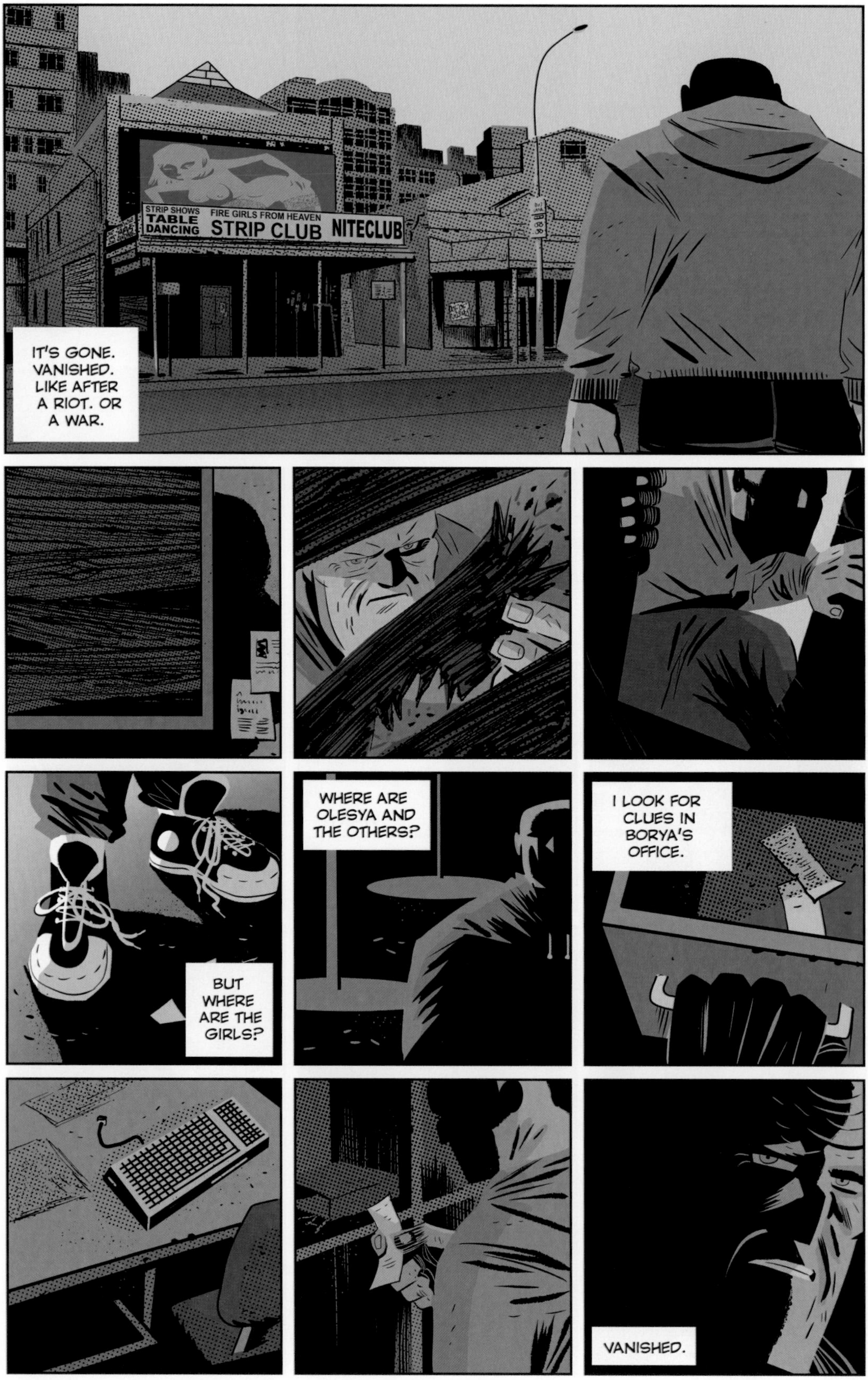
STRIP SHOWS
TABLE DANCING
FIRE GIRLS FROM HEAVEN
STRIP CLUB
NITECLUB
IT'S GONE. VANISHED. LIKE AFTER A RIOT. OR A WAR.
BUT WHERE ARE THE GIRLS?
WHERE ARE OLESYA AND THE OTHERS?
I LOOK FOR CLUES IN BORYA'S OFFICE.
VANISHED.

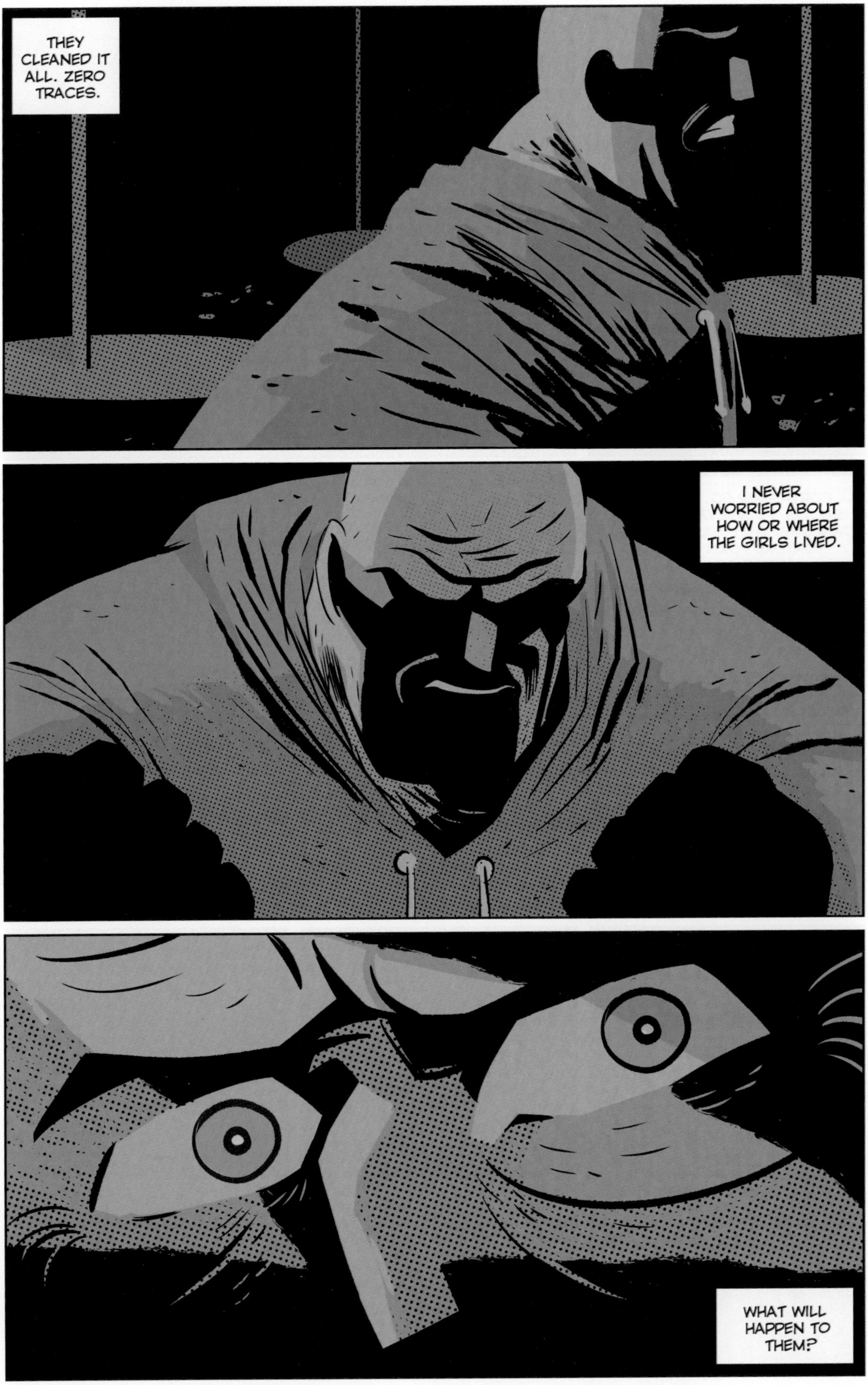
THEY CLEANED IT ALL. ZERO TRACES.
I NEVER WORRIED ABOUT HOW OR WHERE THE GIRLS LIVED.
WHAT WILL HAPPEN TO THEM?

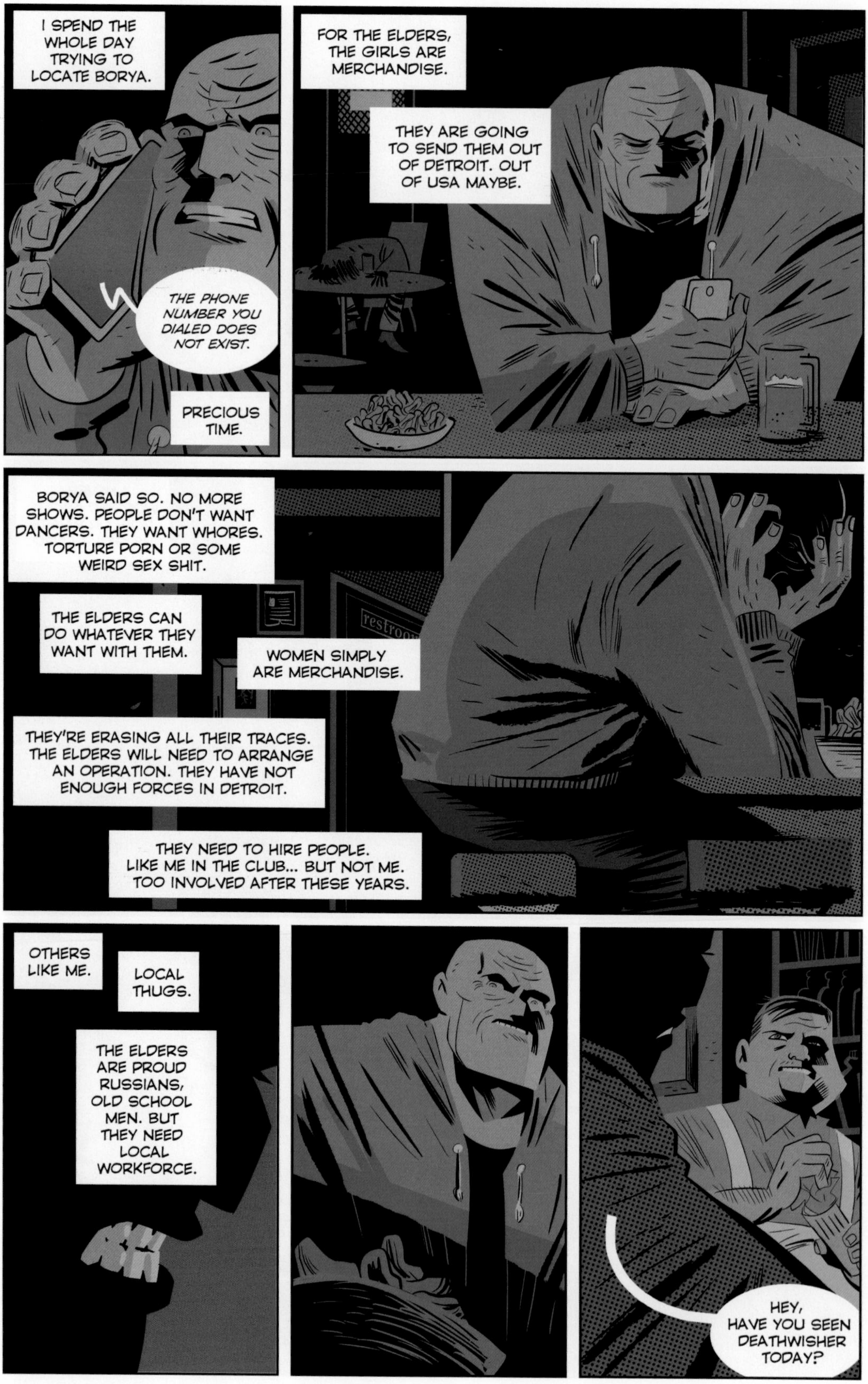

I SPEND THE WHOLE DAY TRYING TO LOCATE BORYA.
THE PHONE NUMBER YOU DIALED DOES NOT EXIST.
PRECIOUS TIME.
FOR THE ELDERS, THE GIRLS ARE MERCHANDISE.
THEY ARE GOING TO SEND THEM OUT OF DETROIT. OUT OF USA MAYBE.
BORYA SAID SO. NO MORE SHOWS. PEOPLE DON'T WANT DANCERS. THEY WANT WHORES. TORTURE PORN OR SOME WEIRD SEX SHIT.
THE ELDERS CAN DO WHATEVER THEY WANT WITH THEM.
WOMEN SIMPLY ARE MERCHANDISE.
restroom
THEY'RE ERASING ALL THEIR TRACES. THE ELDERS WILL NEED TO ARRANGE AN OPERATION. THEY HAVE NOT ENOUGH FORCES IN DETROIT.
THEY NEED TO HIRE PEOPLE. LIKE ME IN THE CLUB... BUT NOT ME. TOO INVOLVED AFTER THESE YEARS.
OTHERS LIKE ME.
LOCAL THUGS.
THE ELDERS ARE PROUD RUSSIANS, OLD SCHOOL MEN. BUT THEY NEED LOCAL WORKFORCE.
HEY, HAVE YOU SEEN DEATHWISHER TODAY?

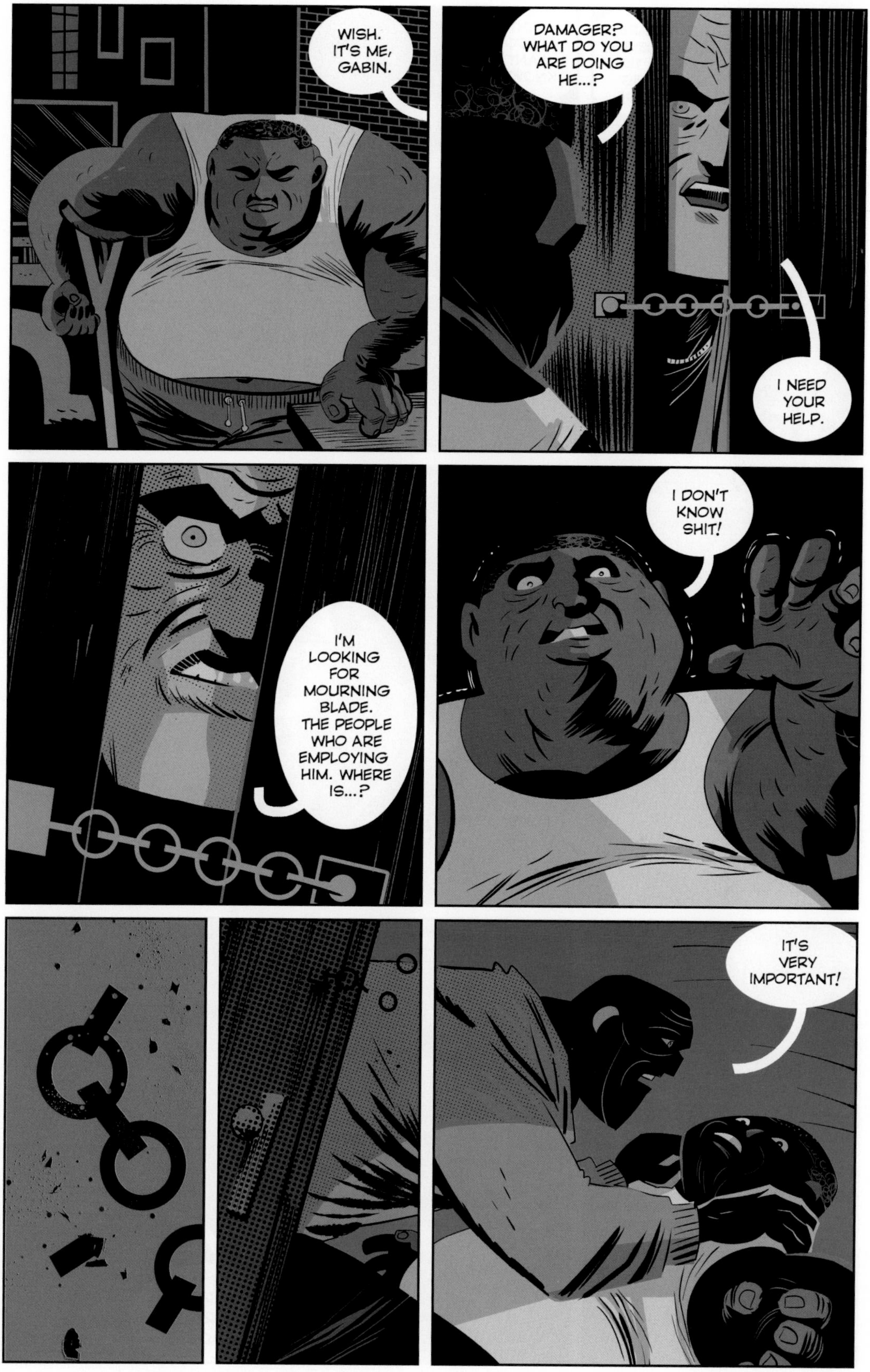
WISH. IT'S ME, GABIN.
DAMAGER? WHAT DO YOU ARE DOING HE...?
I NEED YOUR HELP.
I'M LOOKING FOR MOURNING BLADE. THE PEOPLE WHO ARE EMPLOYING HIM. WHERE IS...?
I DON'T KNOW SHIT!
IT'S VERY IMPORTANT!

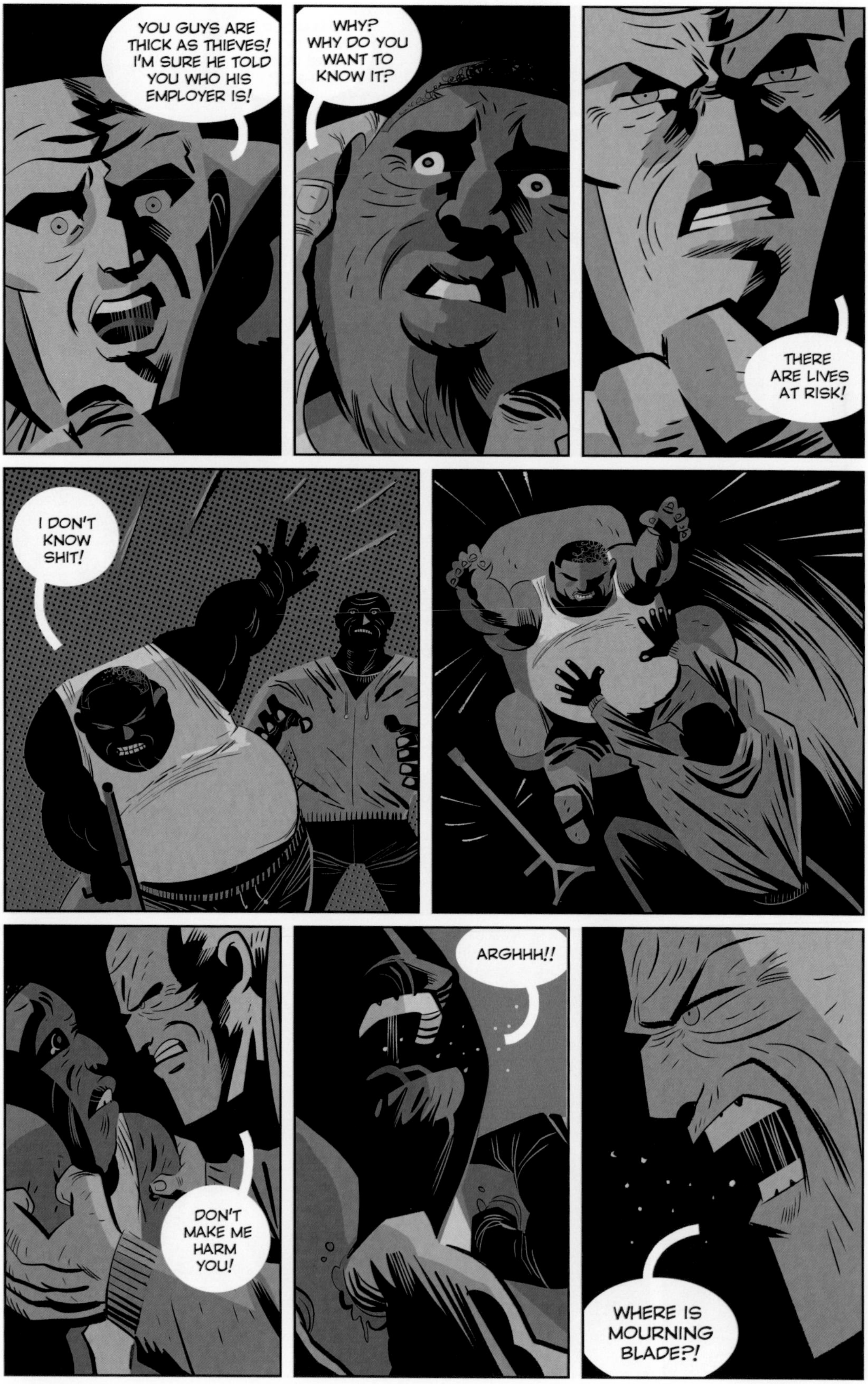

YOU GUYS ARE THICK AS THIEVES! I'M SURE HE TOLD YOU WHO HIS EMPLOYER IS!
WHY? WHY DO YOU WANT TO KNOW IT?
THERE ARE LIVES AT RISK!
I DON'T KNOW SHIT!
DON'T MAKE ME HARM YOU!
ARGHHH!!
WHERE IS MOURNING BLADE?!

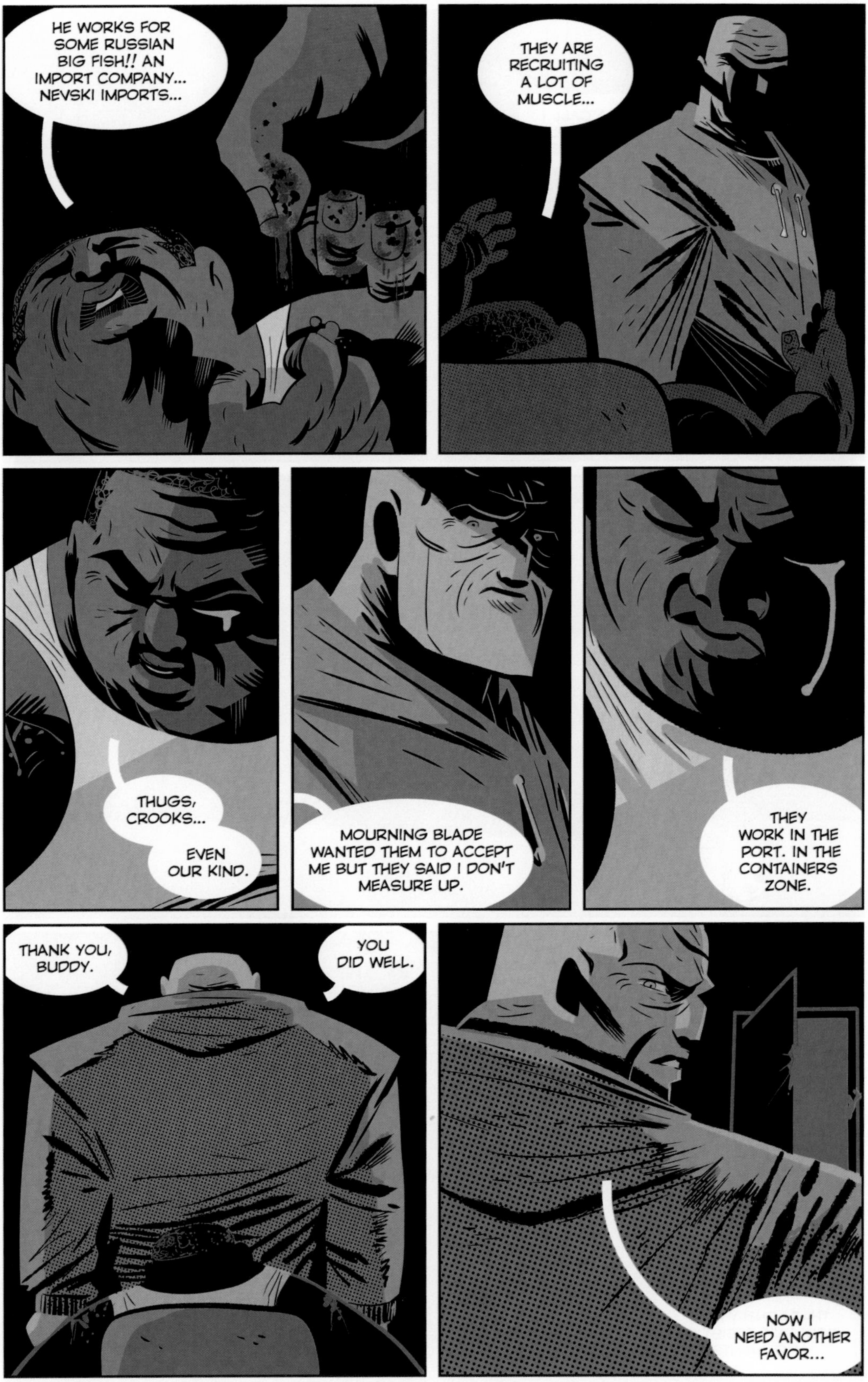

HE WORKS FOR SOME RUSSIAN BIG FISH!! AN IMPORT COMPANY... NEVSKI IMPORTS...
THEY ARE RECRUITING A LOT OF MUSCLE...
THUGS, CROOKS...
EVEN OUR KIND.
MOURNING BLADE WANTED THEM TO ACCEPT ME BUT THEY SAID I DON'T MEASURE UP.
THEY WORK IN THE PORT. IN THE CONTAINERS ZONE.
THANK YOU, BUDDY.
YOU DID WELL.
NOW I NEED ANOTHER FAVOR...

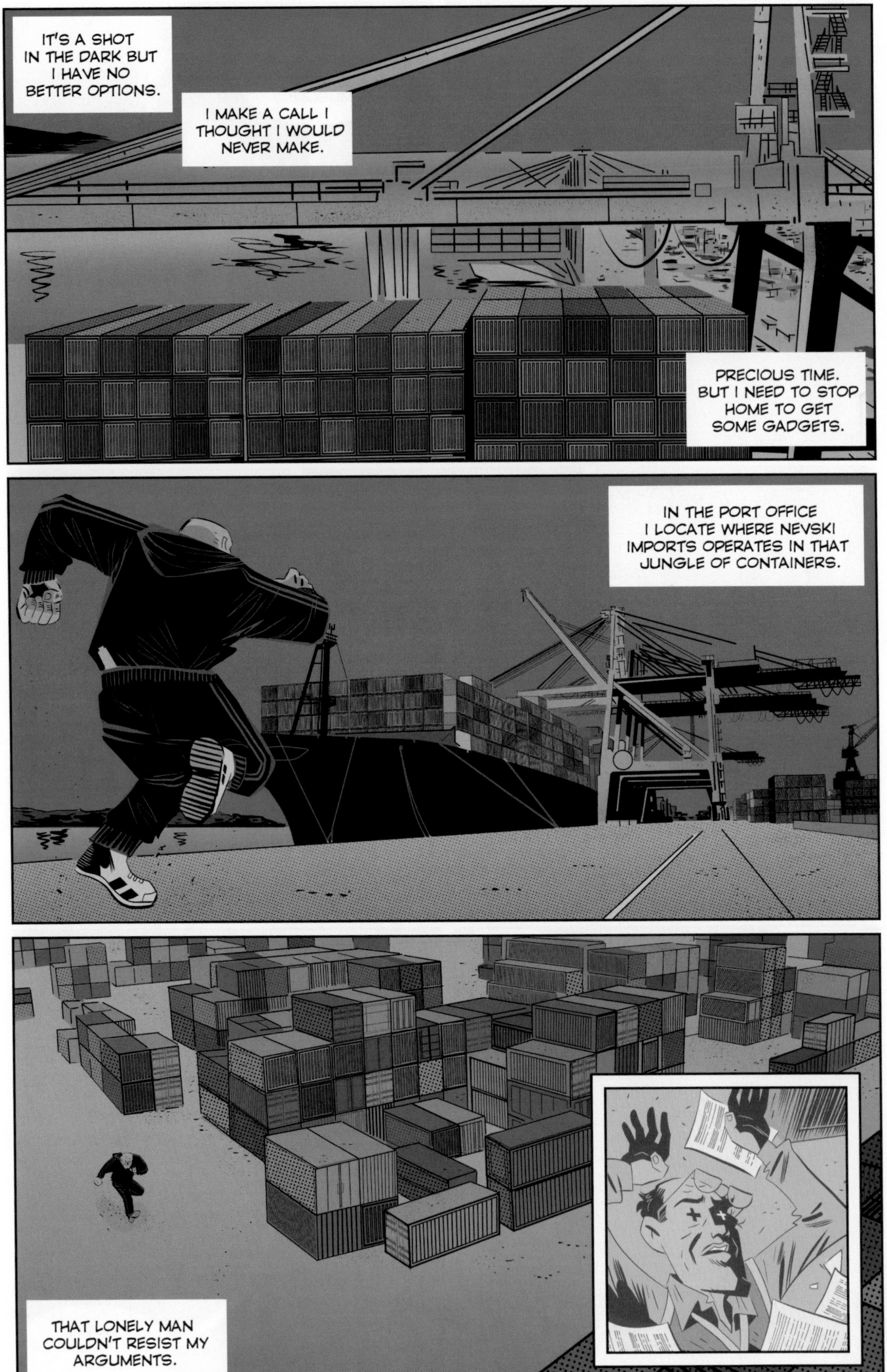
IT'S A SHOT IN THE DARK BUT I HAVE NO BETTER OPTIONS.
I MAKE A CALL I THOUGHT I WOULD NEVER MAKE.
PRECIOUS TIME. BUT I NEED TO STOP HOME TO GET SOME GADGETS.
IN THE PORT OFFICE I LOCATE WHERE NEVSKI IMPORTS OPERATES IN THAT JUNGLE OF CONTAINERS.
THAT LONELY MAN COULDN'T RESIST MY ARGUMENTS.

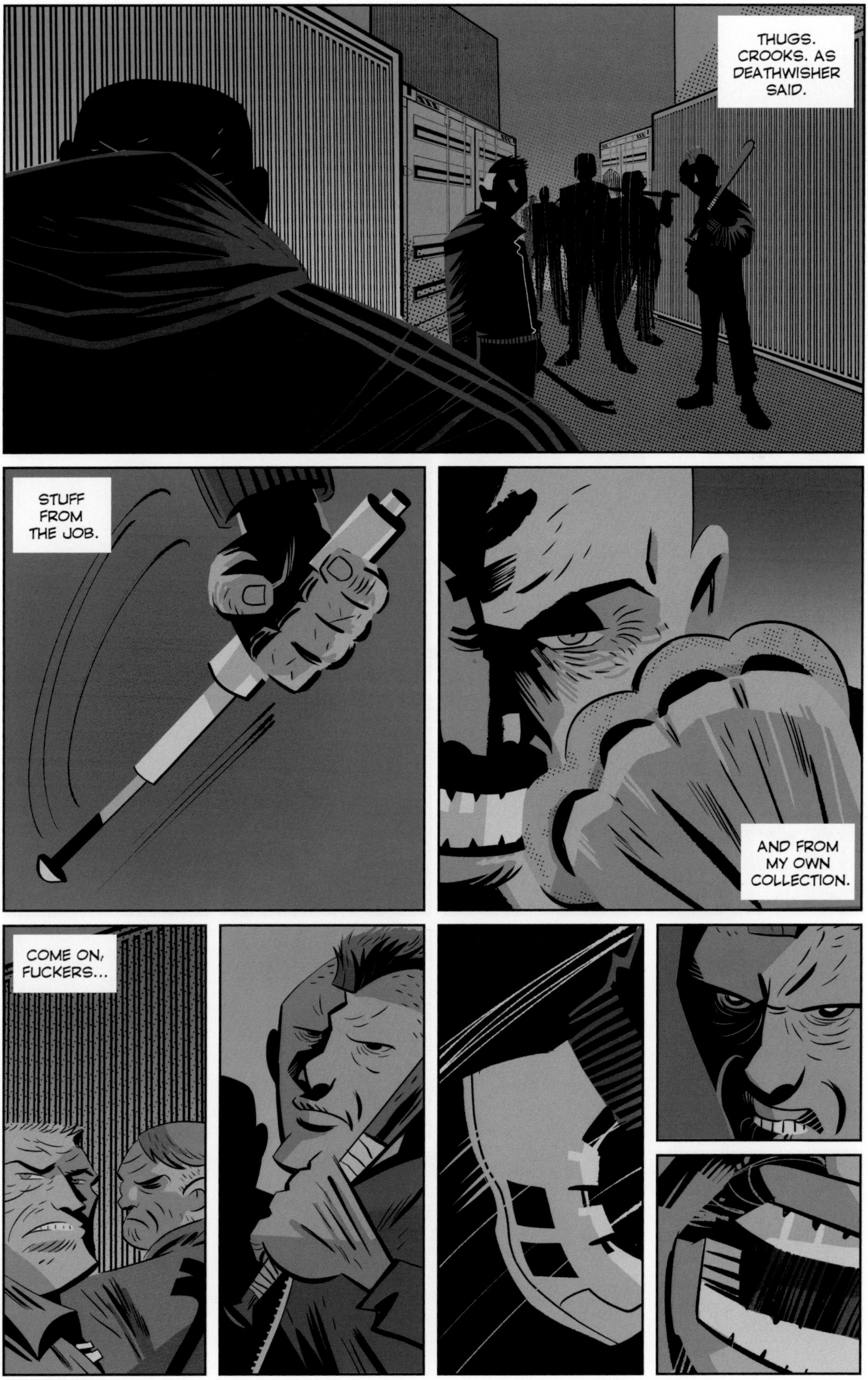
THUGS. CROOKS. AS DEATHWISHER SAID.
STUFF FROM THE JOB.
AND FROM MY OWN COLLECTION.
COME ON, FUCKERS...

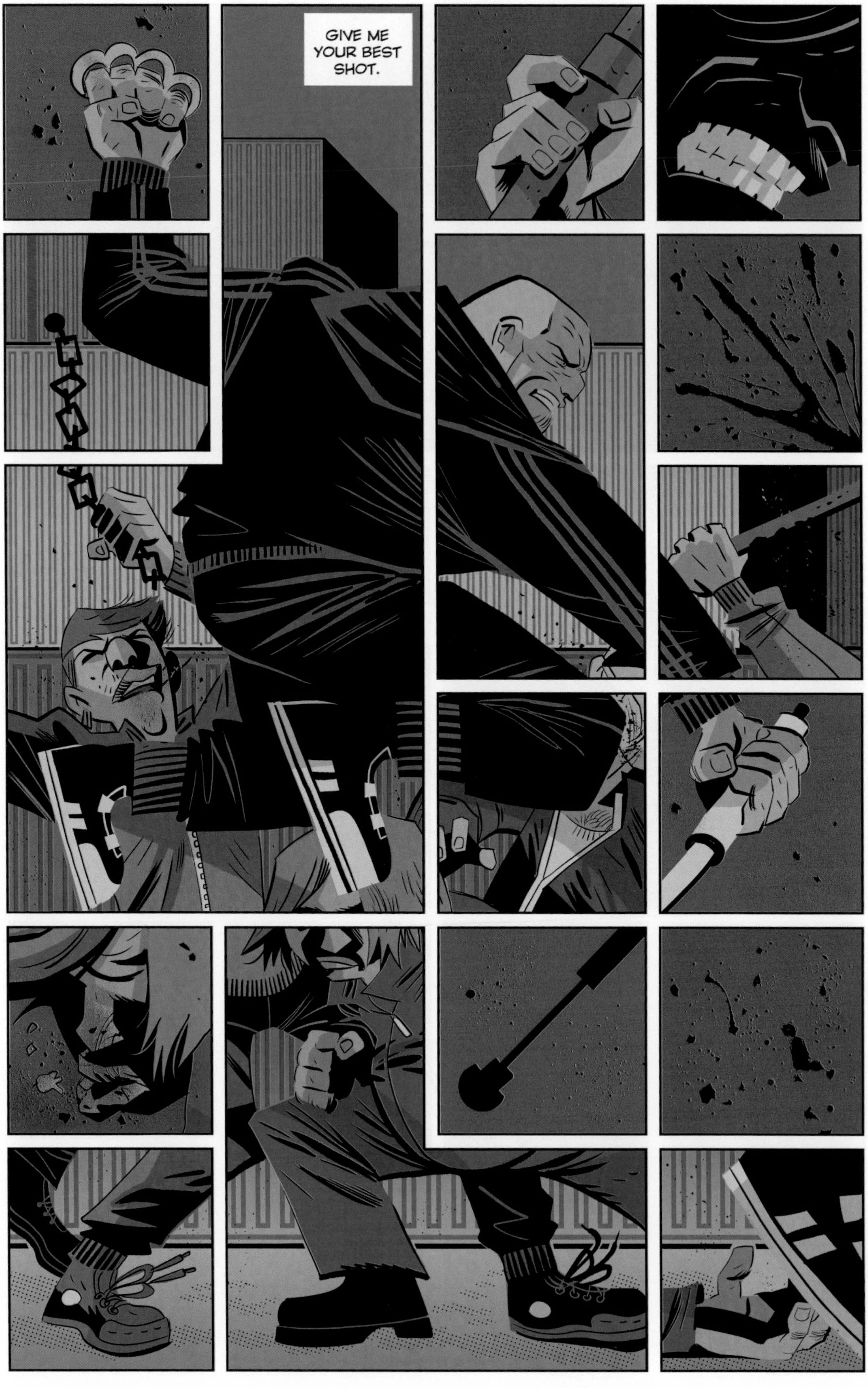
GIVE ME YOUR BEST SHOT.

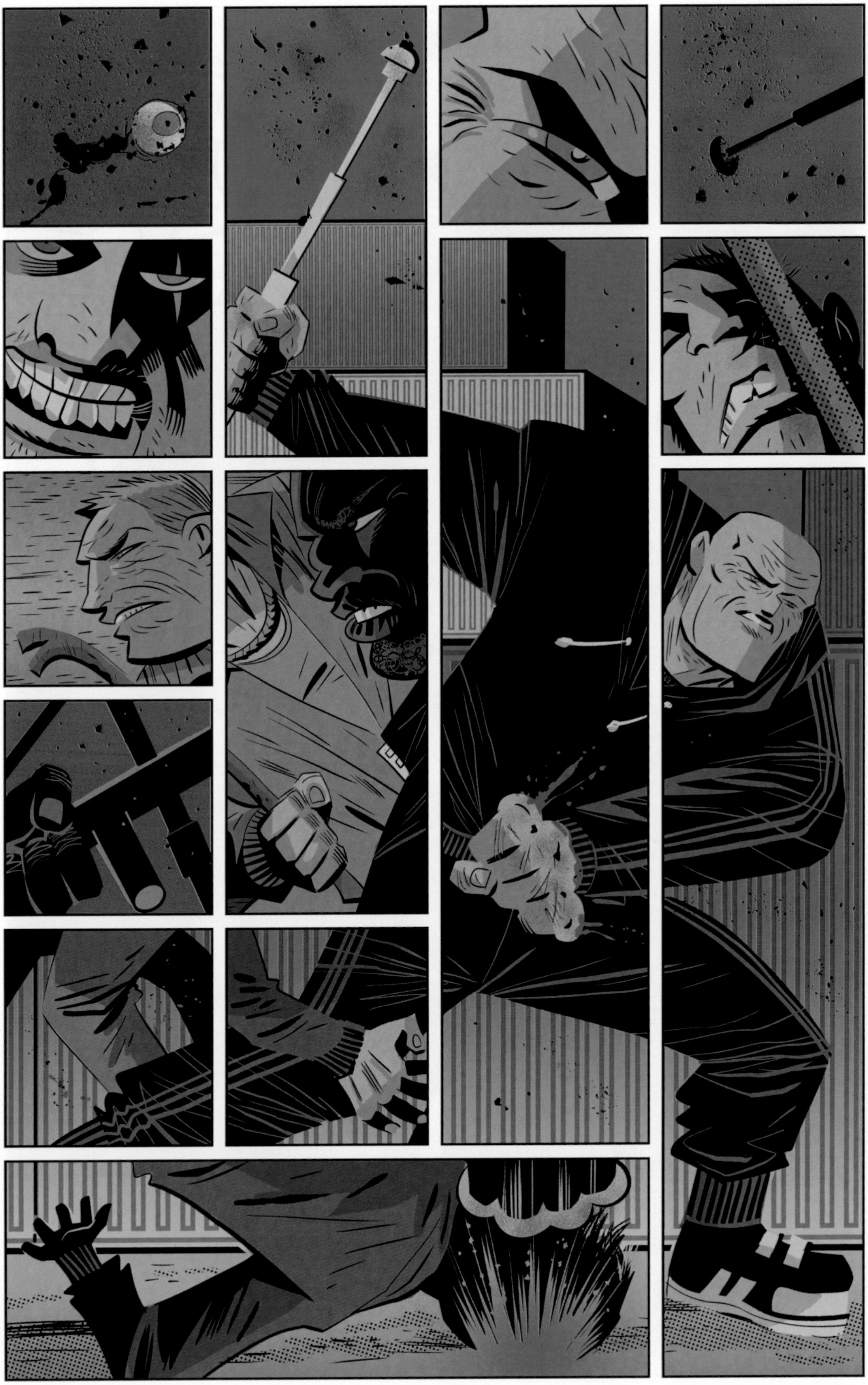

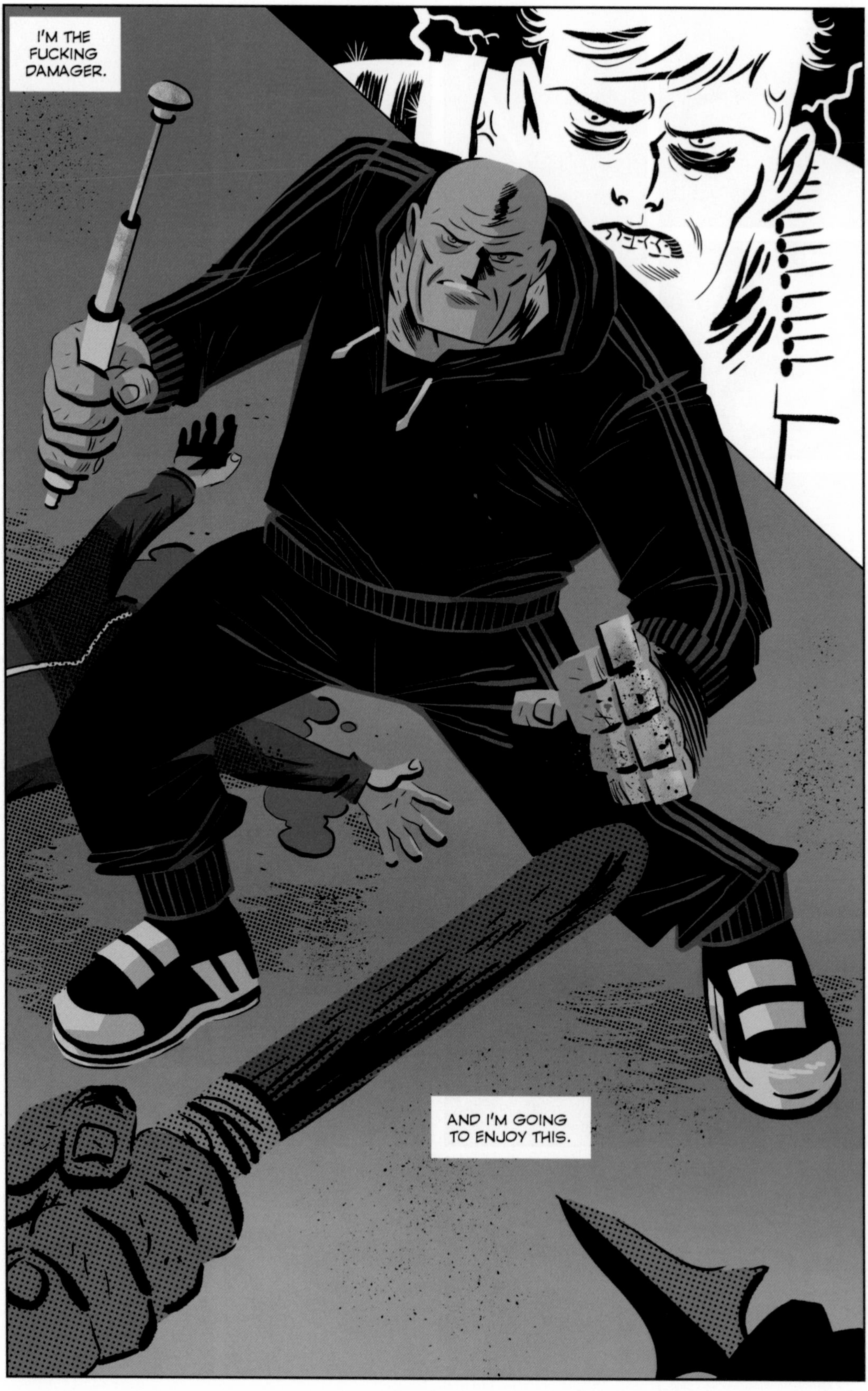
I'M THE FUCKING DAMAGER.
AND I'M GOING TO ENJOY THIS.

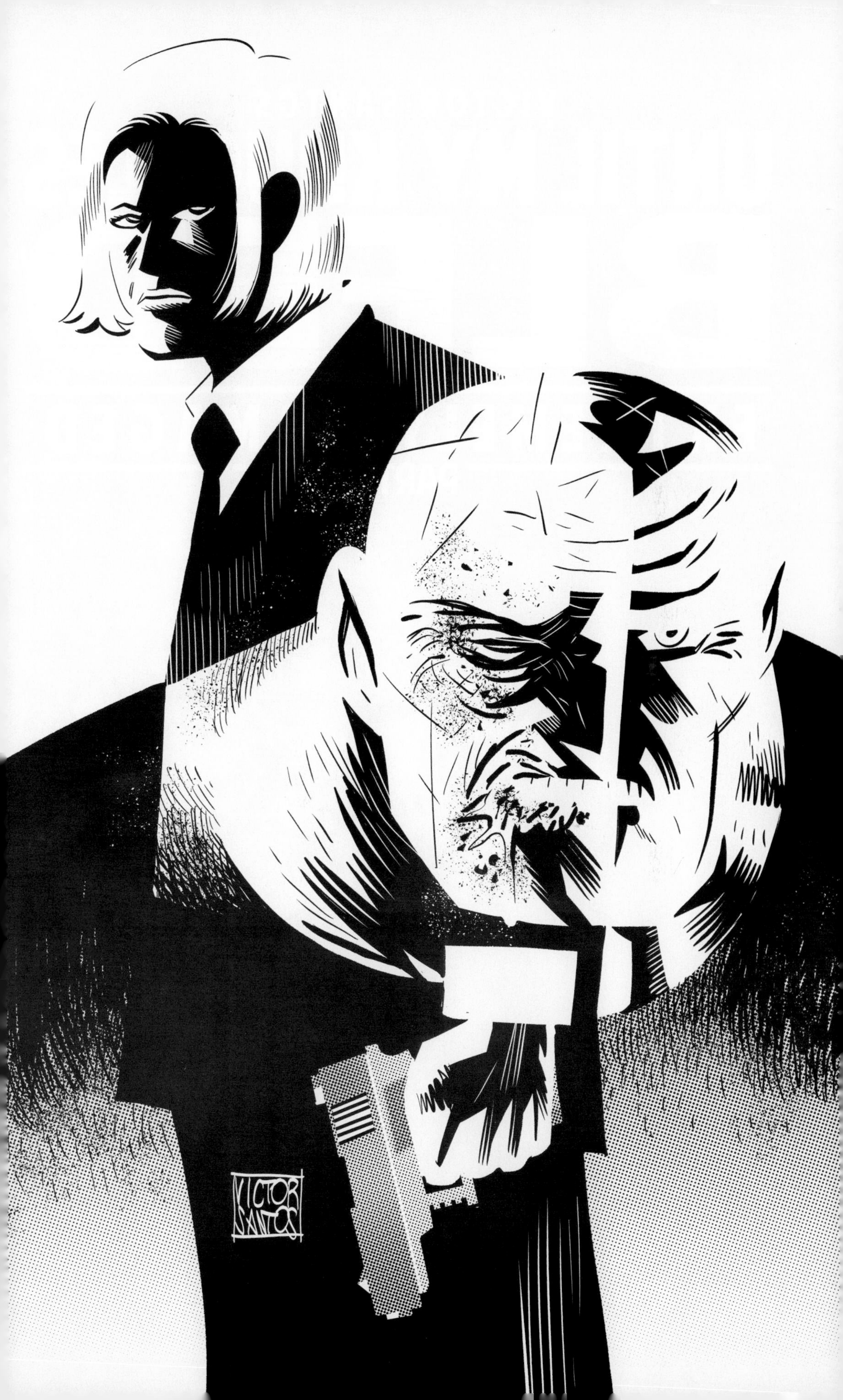
VICTOR SANTOS

VICTOR SANTOS

# UNTIL MY KNUCKLES BLEED

## EXTREMELY DAMAGED

### PART 3

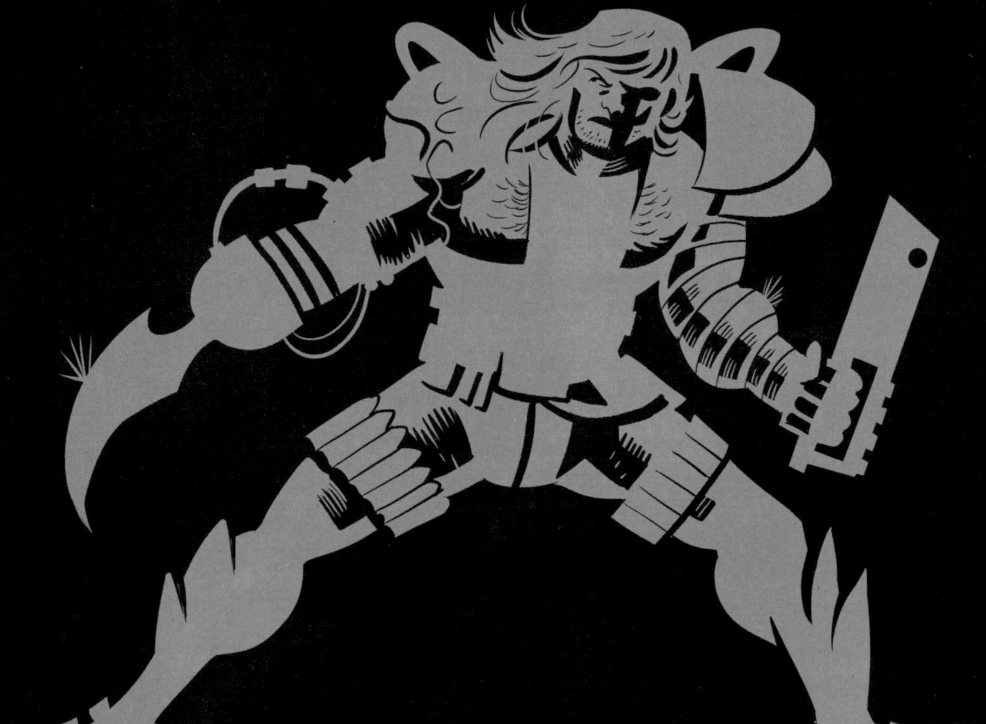

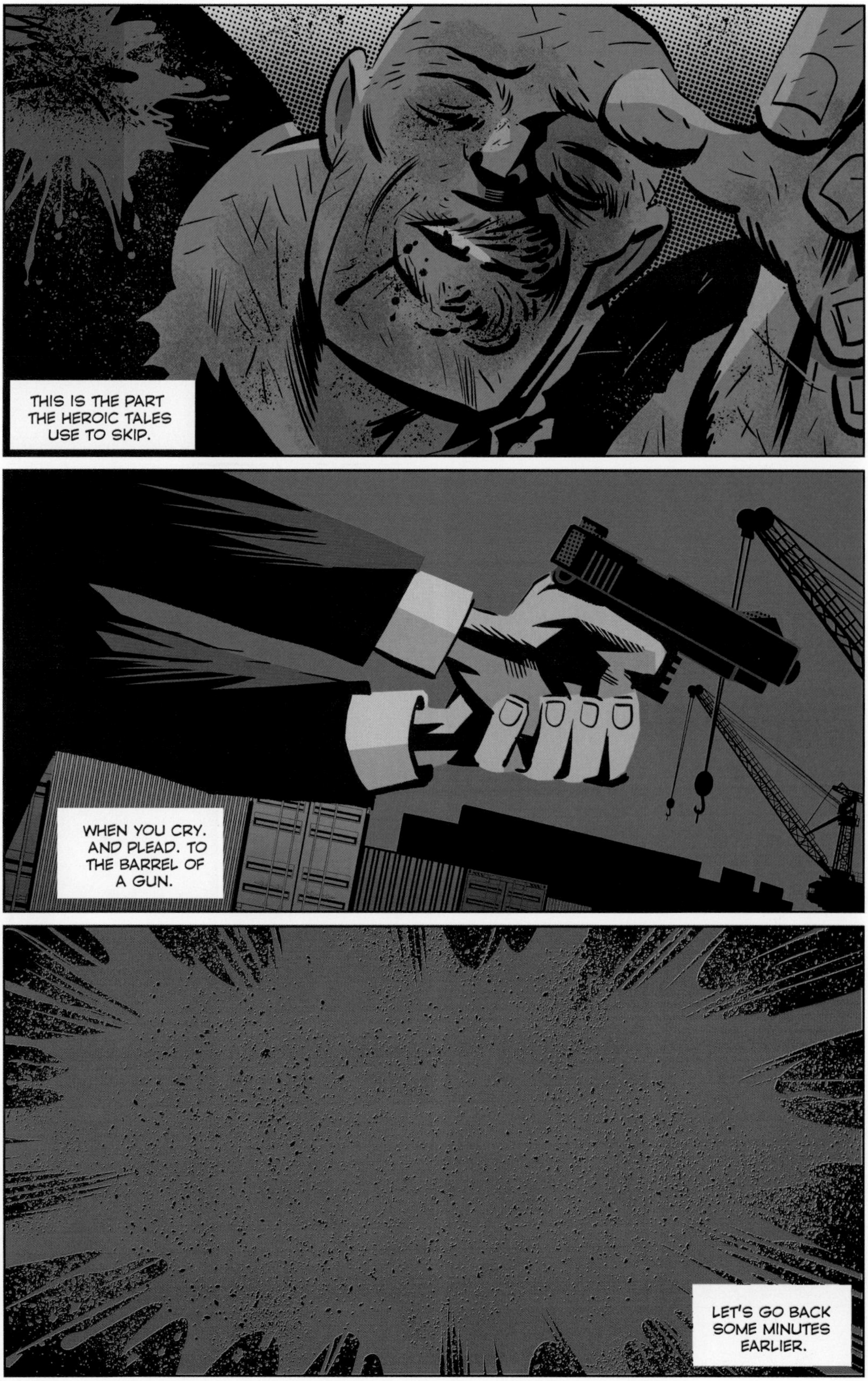
THIS IS THE PART THE HEROIC TALES USE TO SKIP.
WHEN YOU CRY. AND PLEAD. TO THE BARREL OF A GUN.
LET'S GO BACK SOME MINUTES EARLIER.

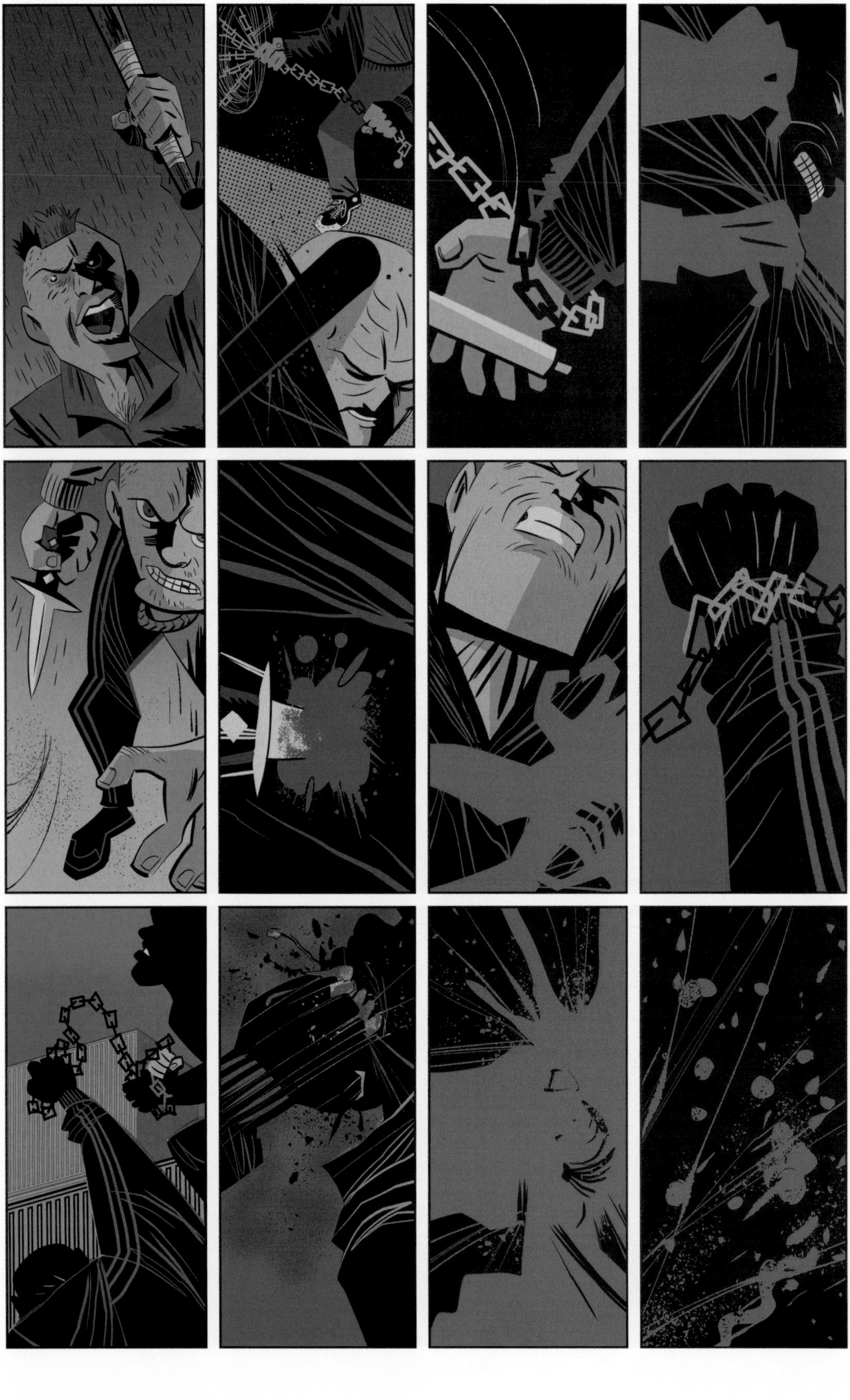

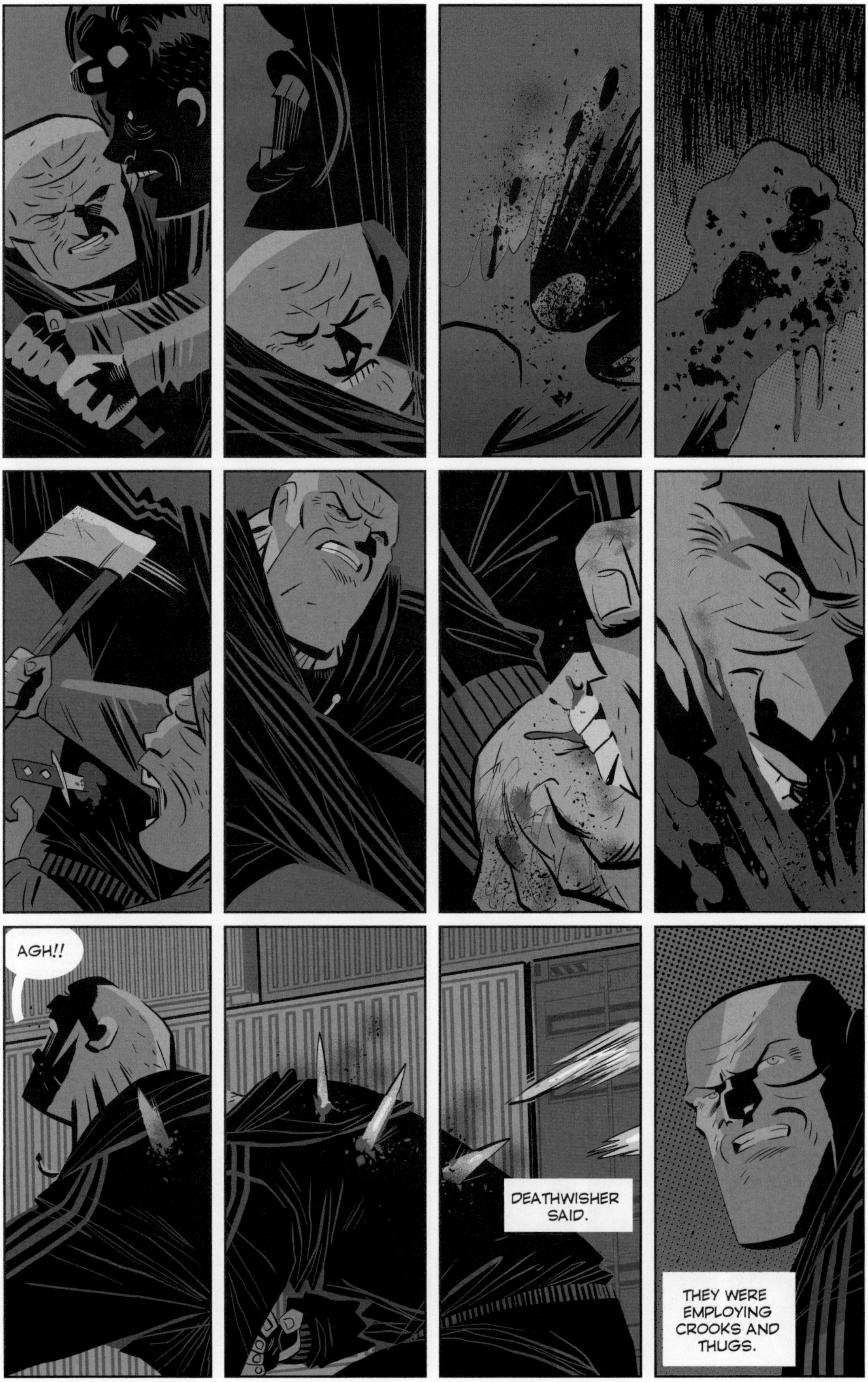
AGH!!
DEATHWISHER SAID.
THEY WERE EMPLOYING CROOKS AND THUGS.

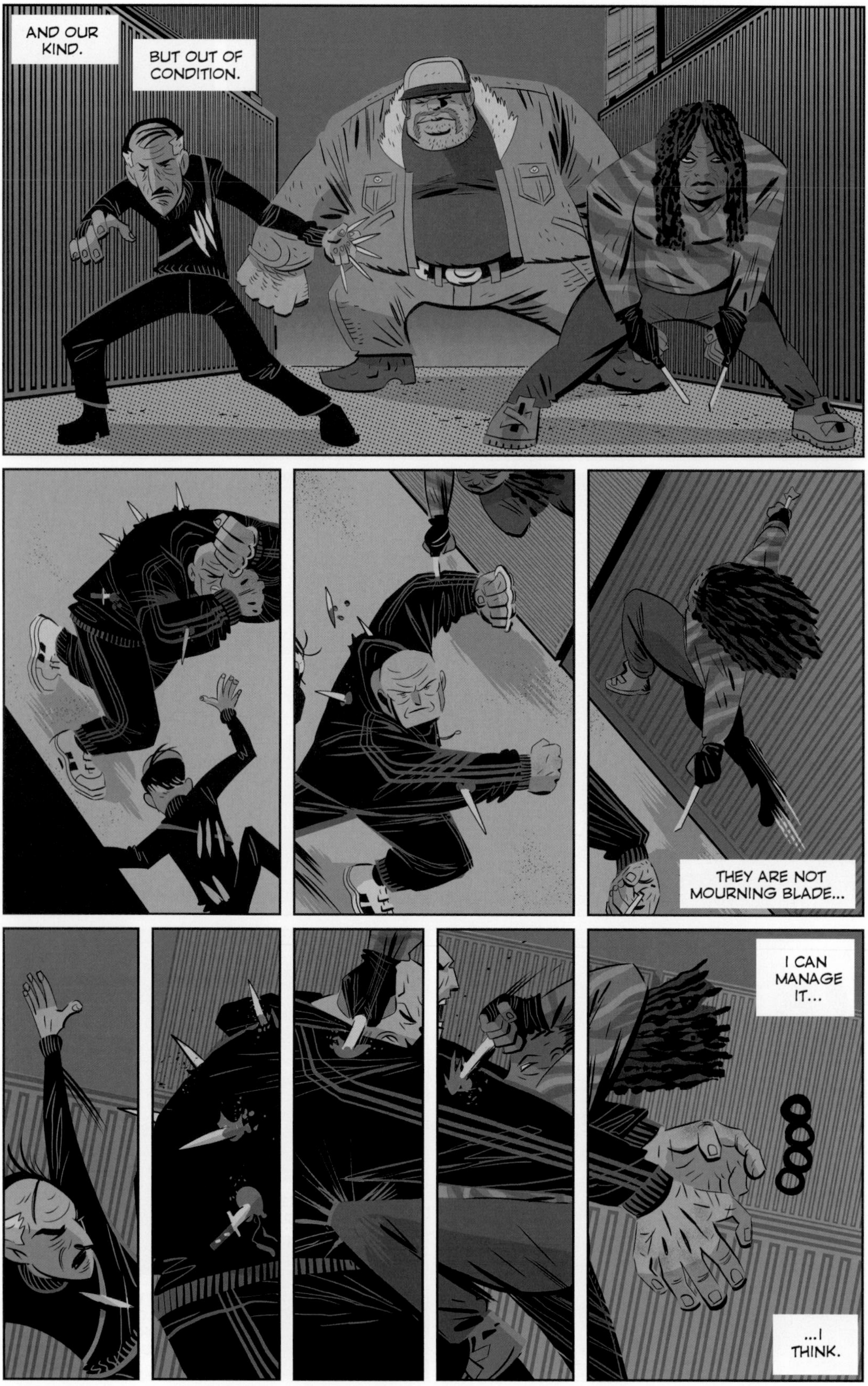
AND OUR KIND.
BUT OUT OF CONDITION.
THEY ARE NOT MOURNING BLADE...
I CAN MANAGE IT...
...I THINK.

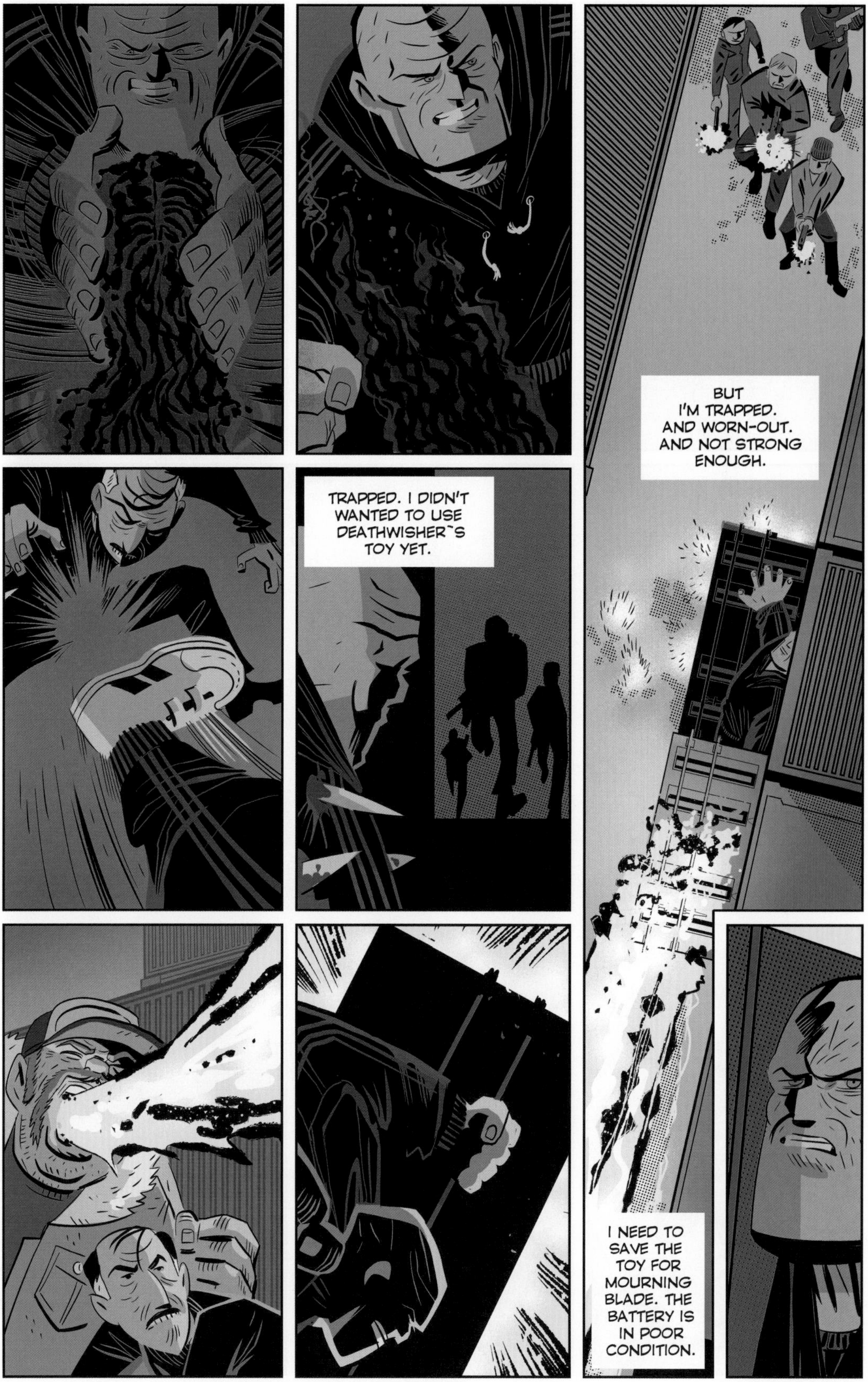
BUT I'M TRAPPED. AND WORN-OUT. AND NOT STRONG ENOUGH.
TRAPPED. I DIDN'T WANTED TO USE DEATHWISHER~S TOY YET.
I NEED TO SAVE THE TOY FOR MOURNING BLADE. THE BATTERY IS IN POOR CONDITION.

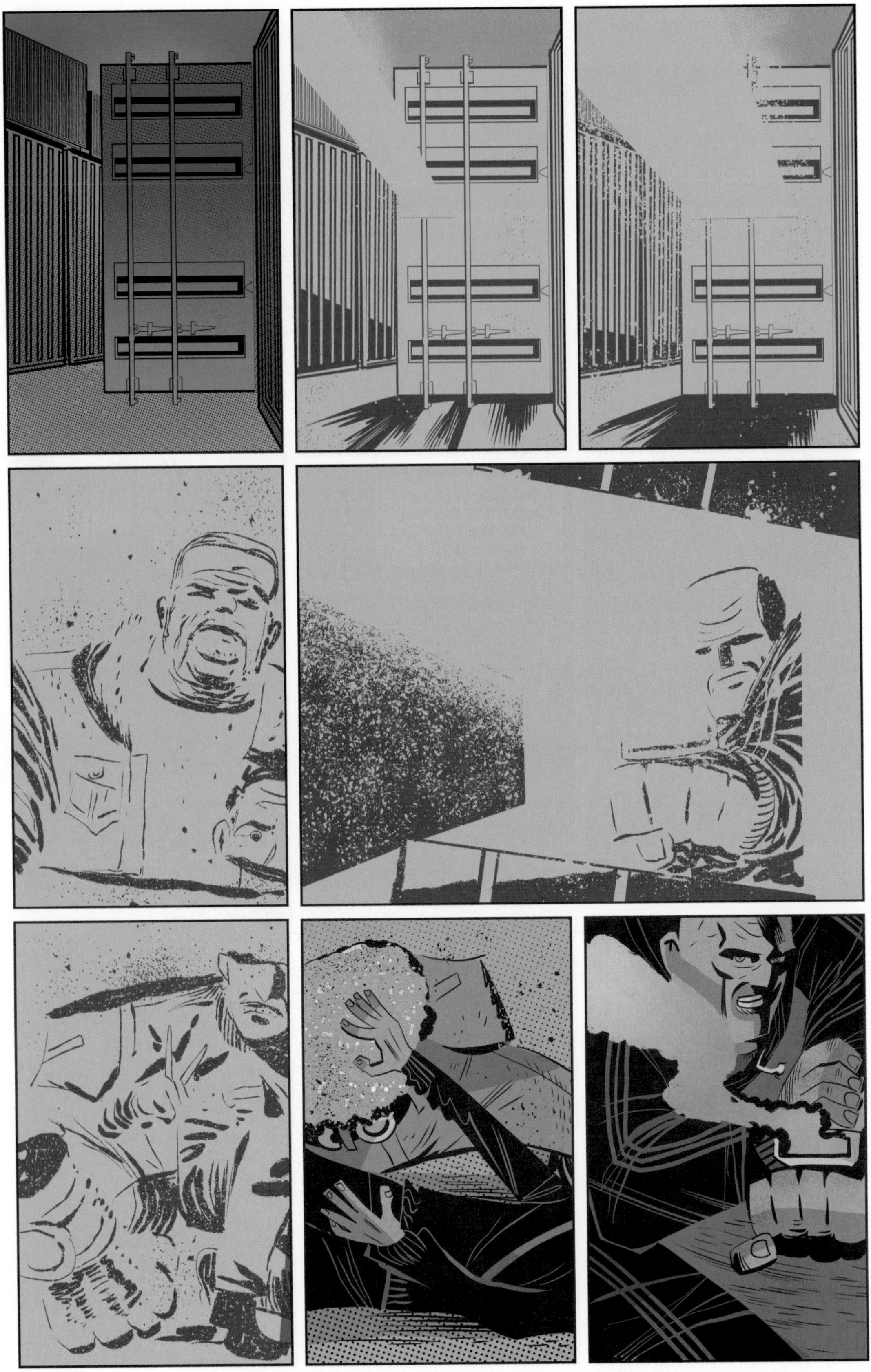

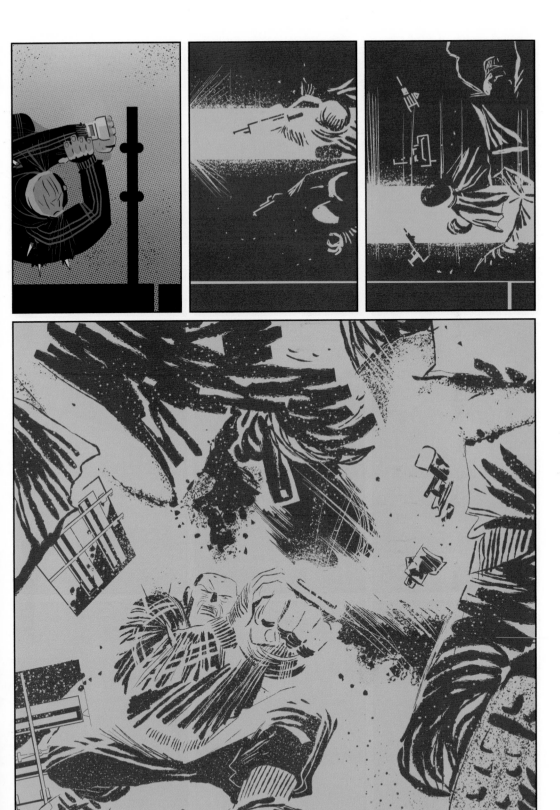

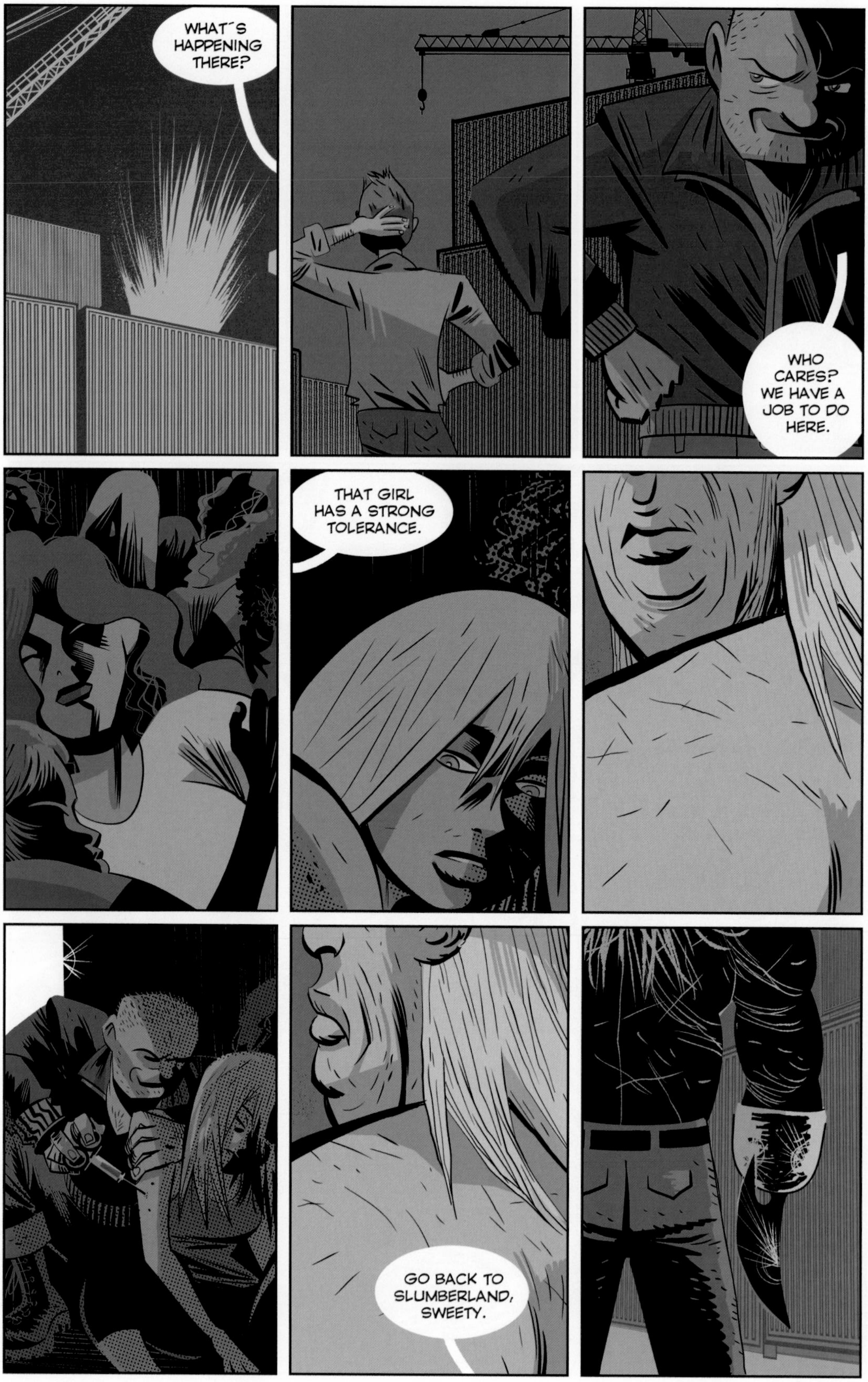
WHAT´S HAPPENING THERE?
WHO CARES? WE HAVE A JOB TO DO HERE.
THAT GIRL HAS A STRONG TOLERANCE.
GO BACK TO SLUMBERLAND, SWEETY.

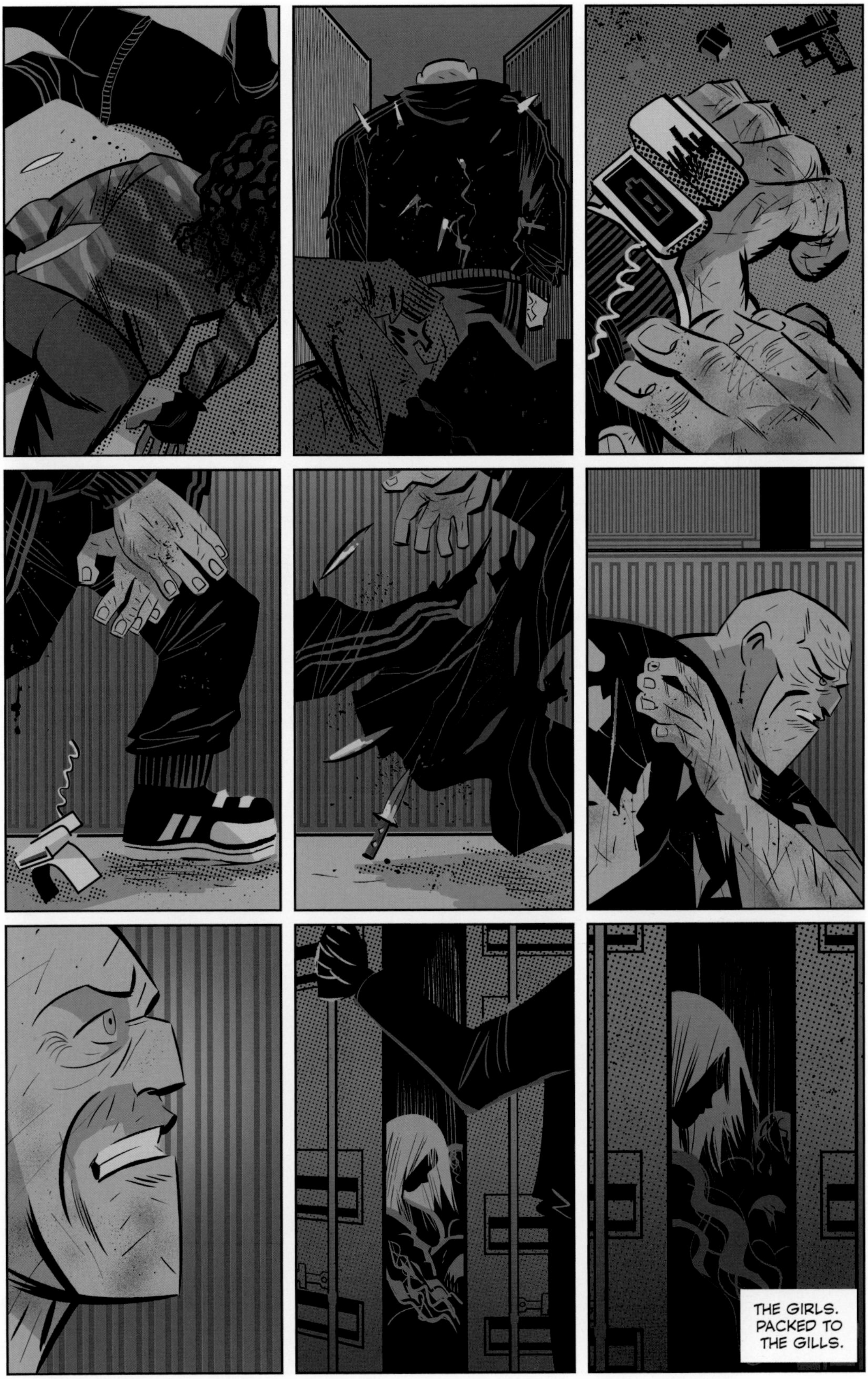
THE GIRLS.
PACKED TO
THE GILLS.

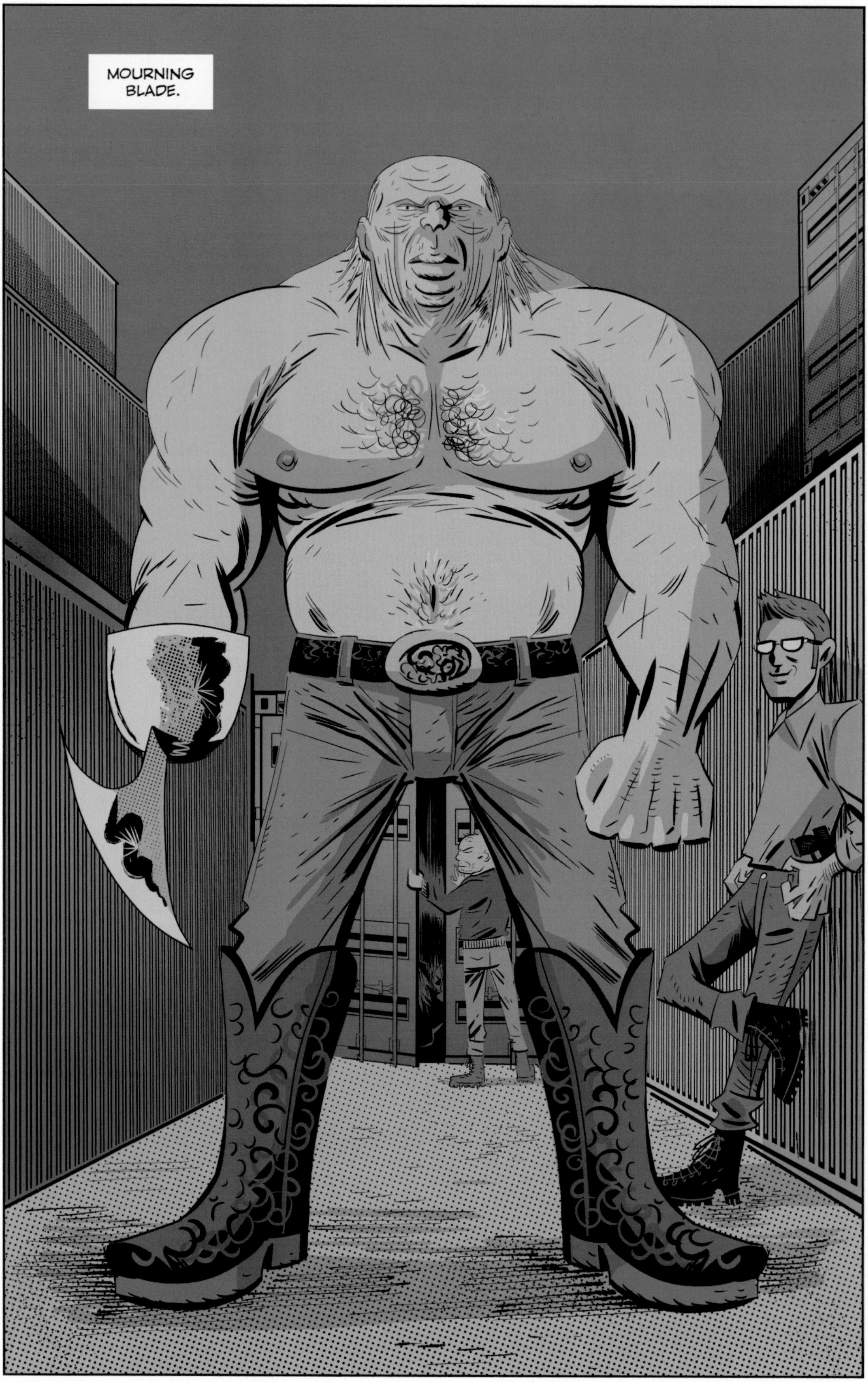
MOURNING
BLADE.

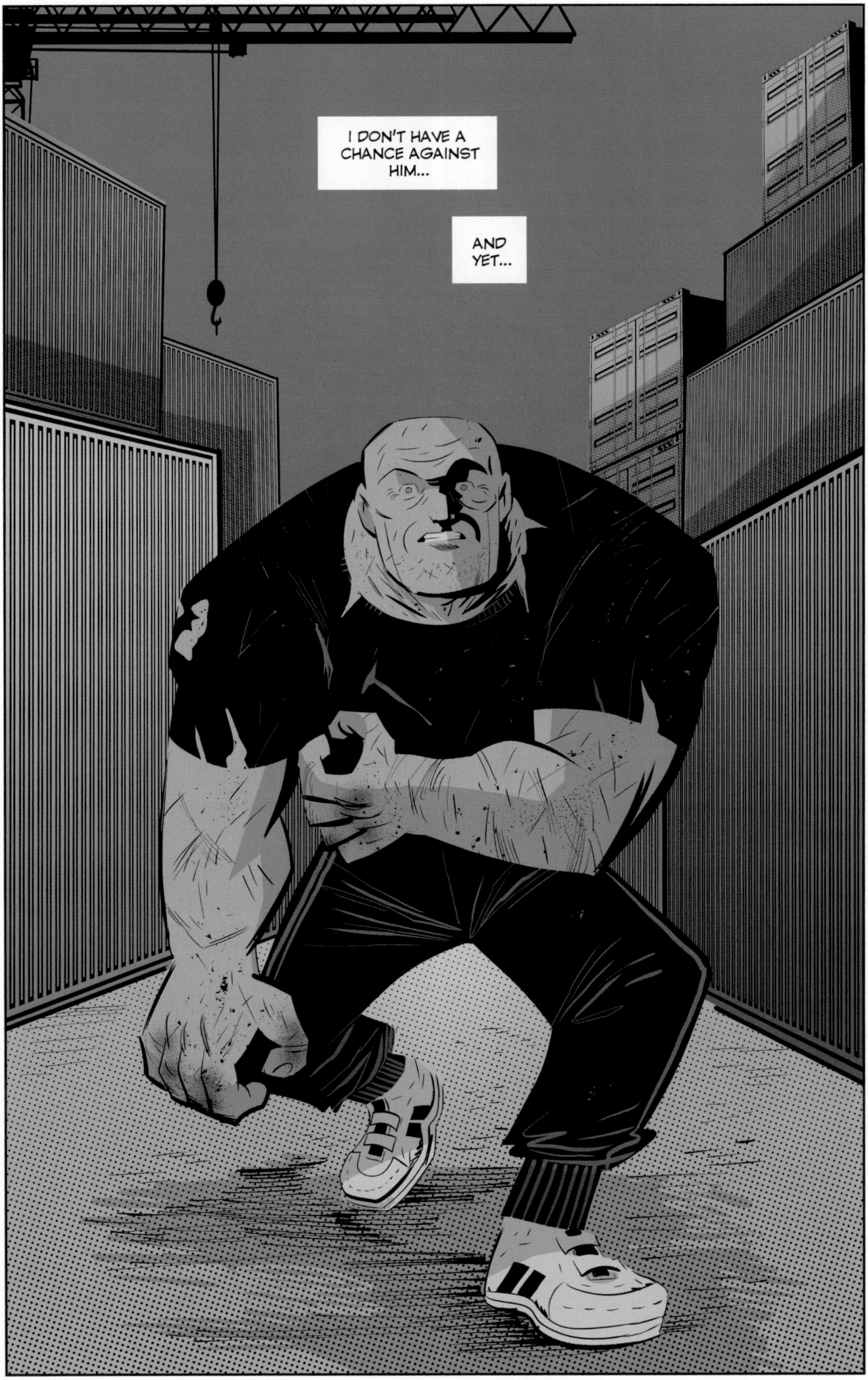
I DON'T HAVE A CHANCE AGAINST HIM...
AND YET...

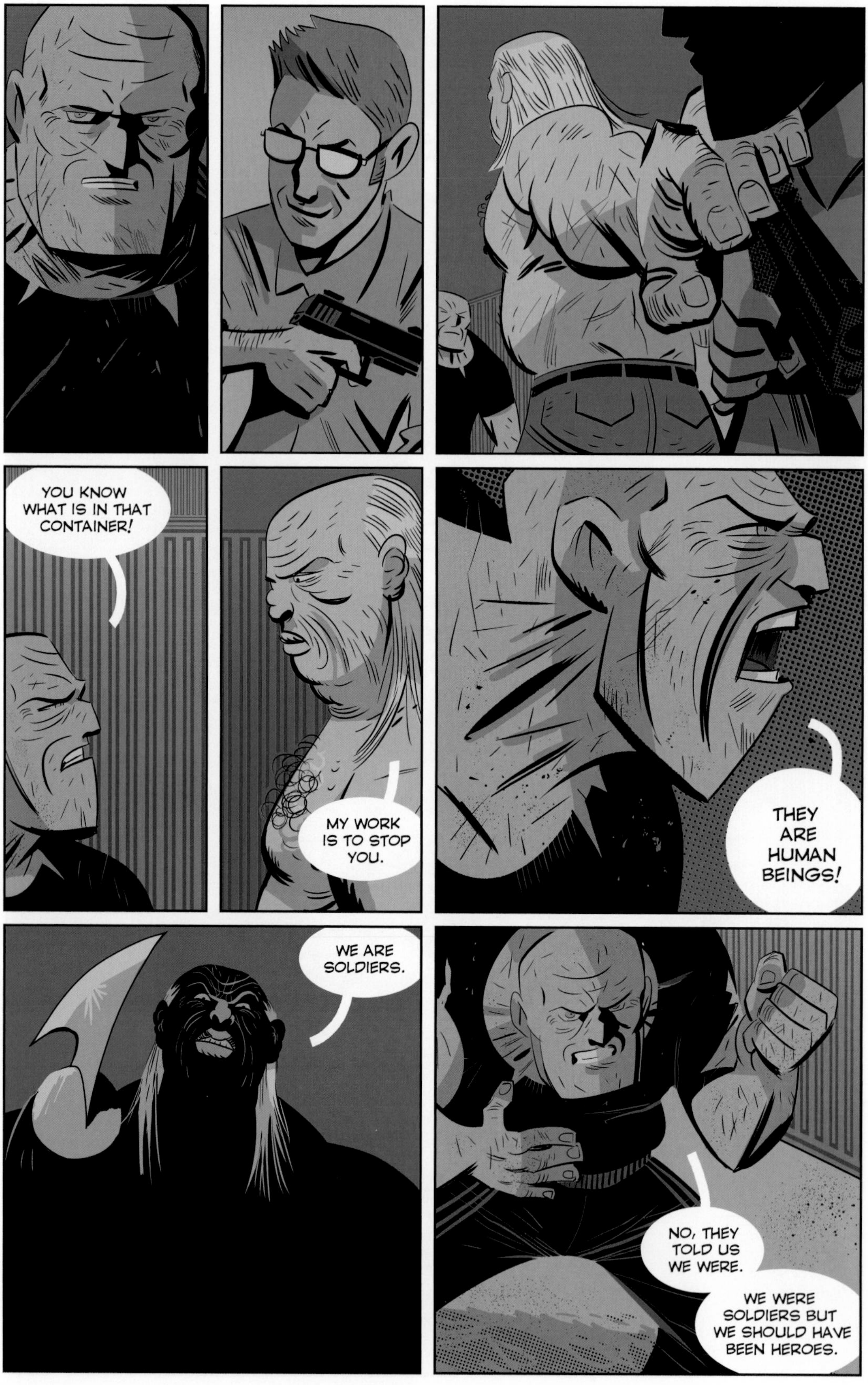
YOU KNOW WHAT IS IN THAT CONTAINER!
MY WORK IS TO STOP YOU.
THEY ARE HUMAN BEINGS!
WE ARE SOLDIERS.
NO, THEY TOLD US WE WERE.
WE WERE SOLDIERS BUT WE SHOULD HAVE BEEN HEROES.

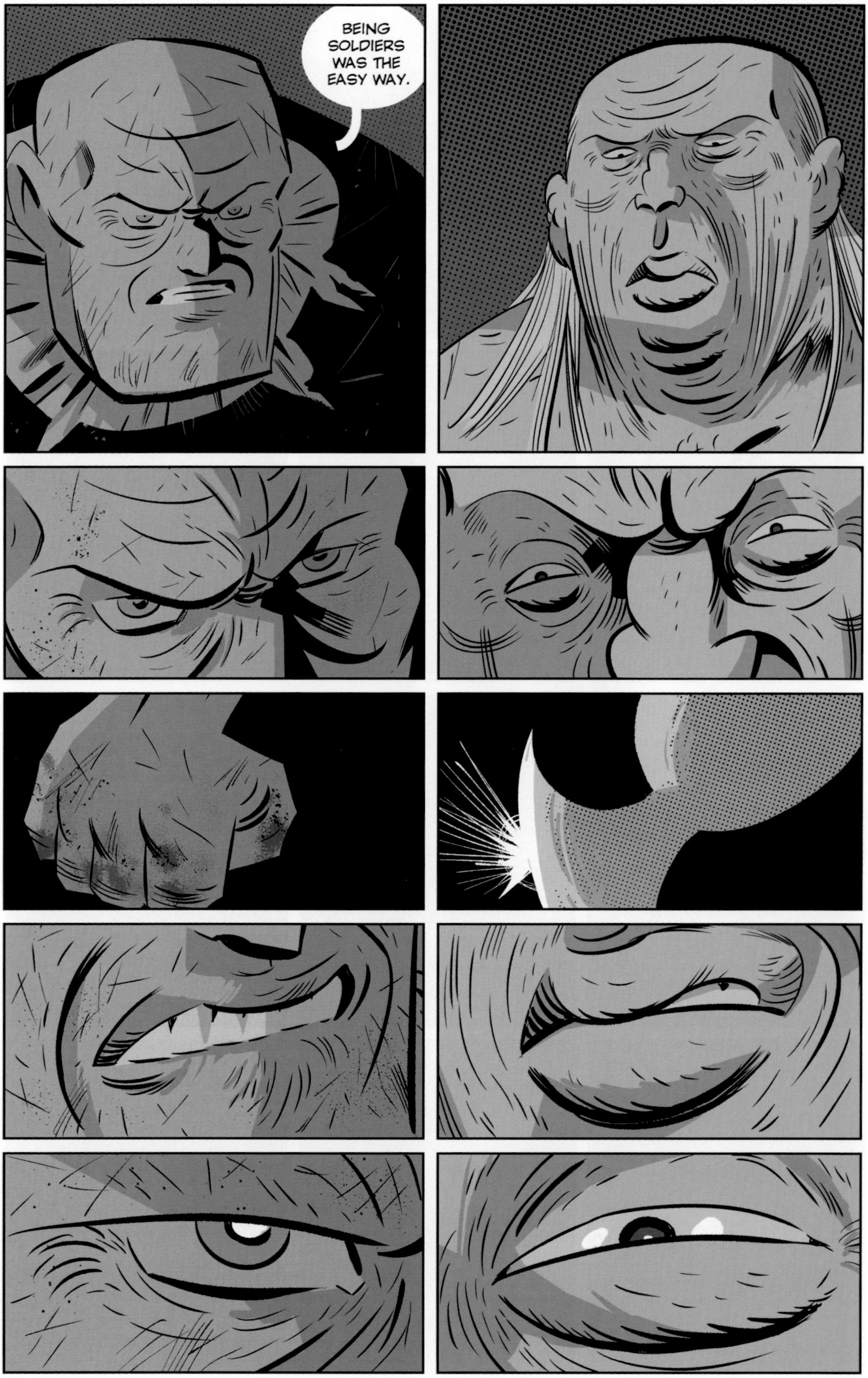
BEING SOLDIERS WAS THE EASY WAY.

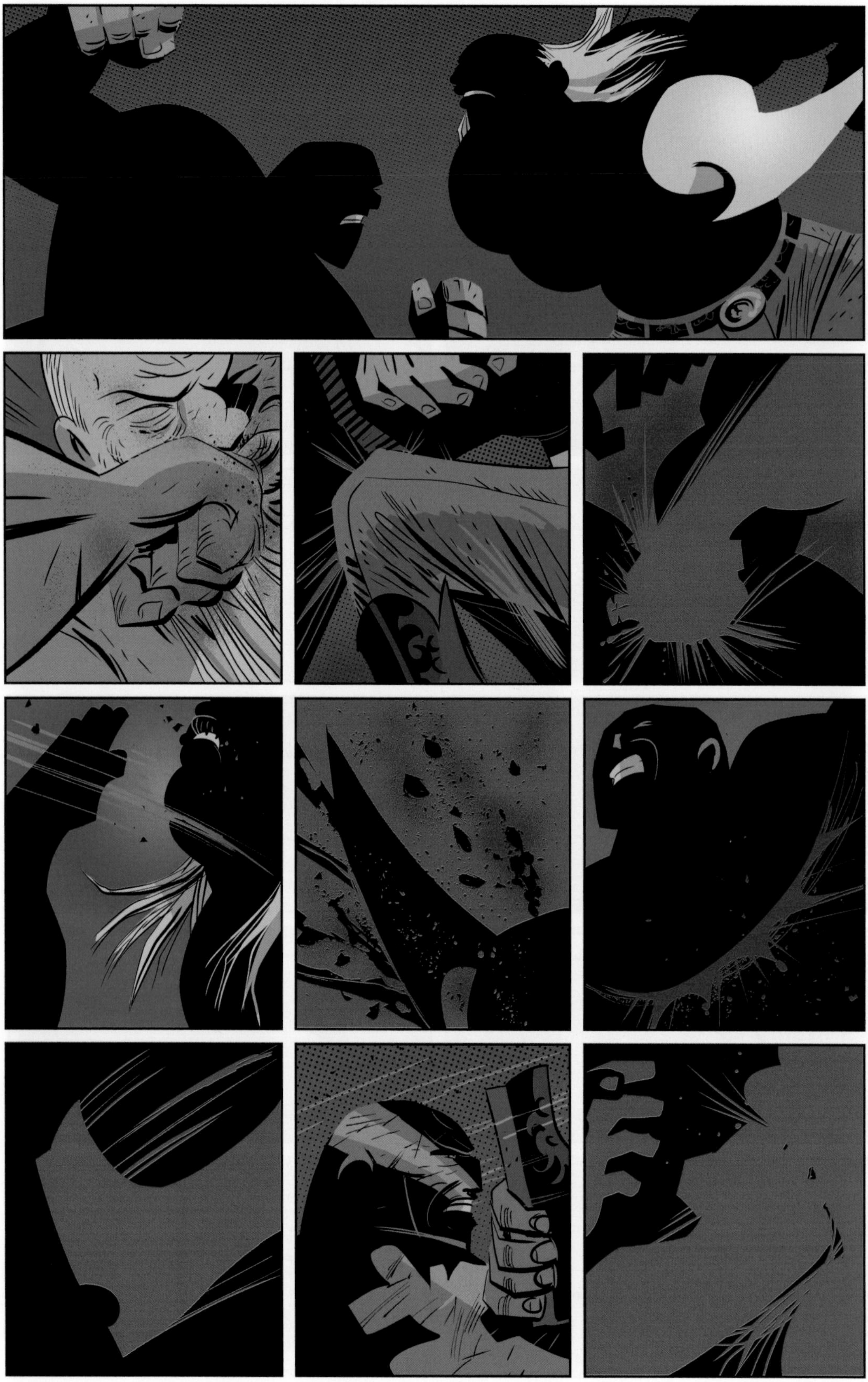

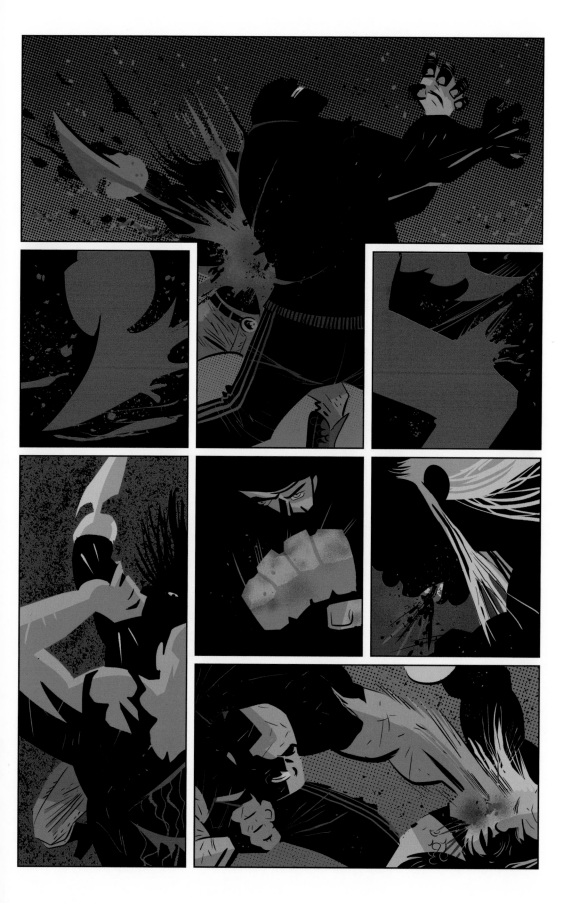

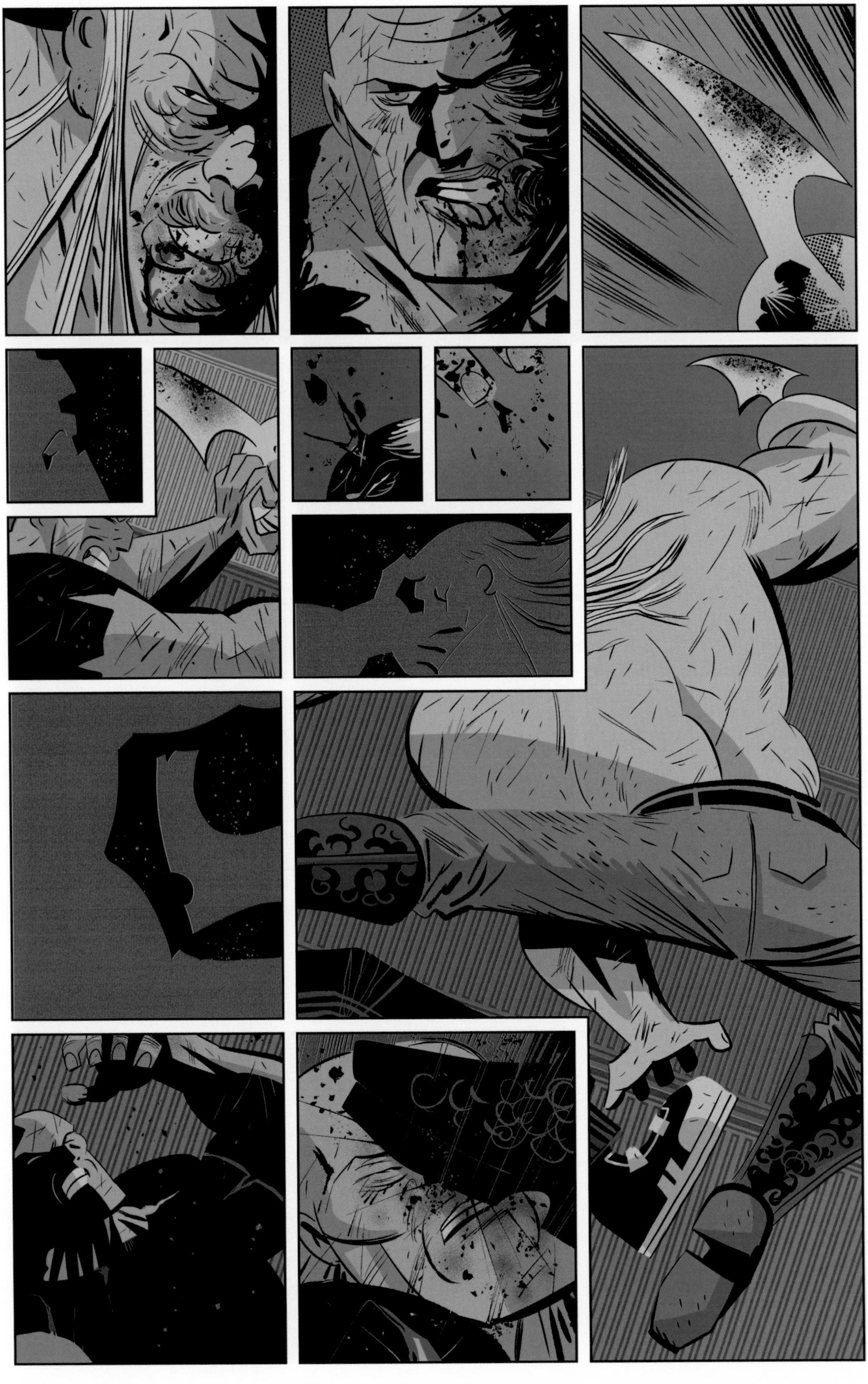

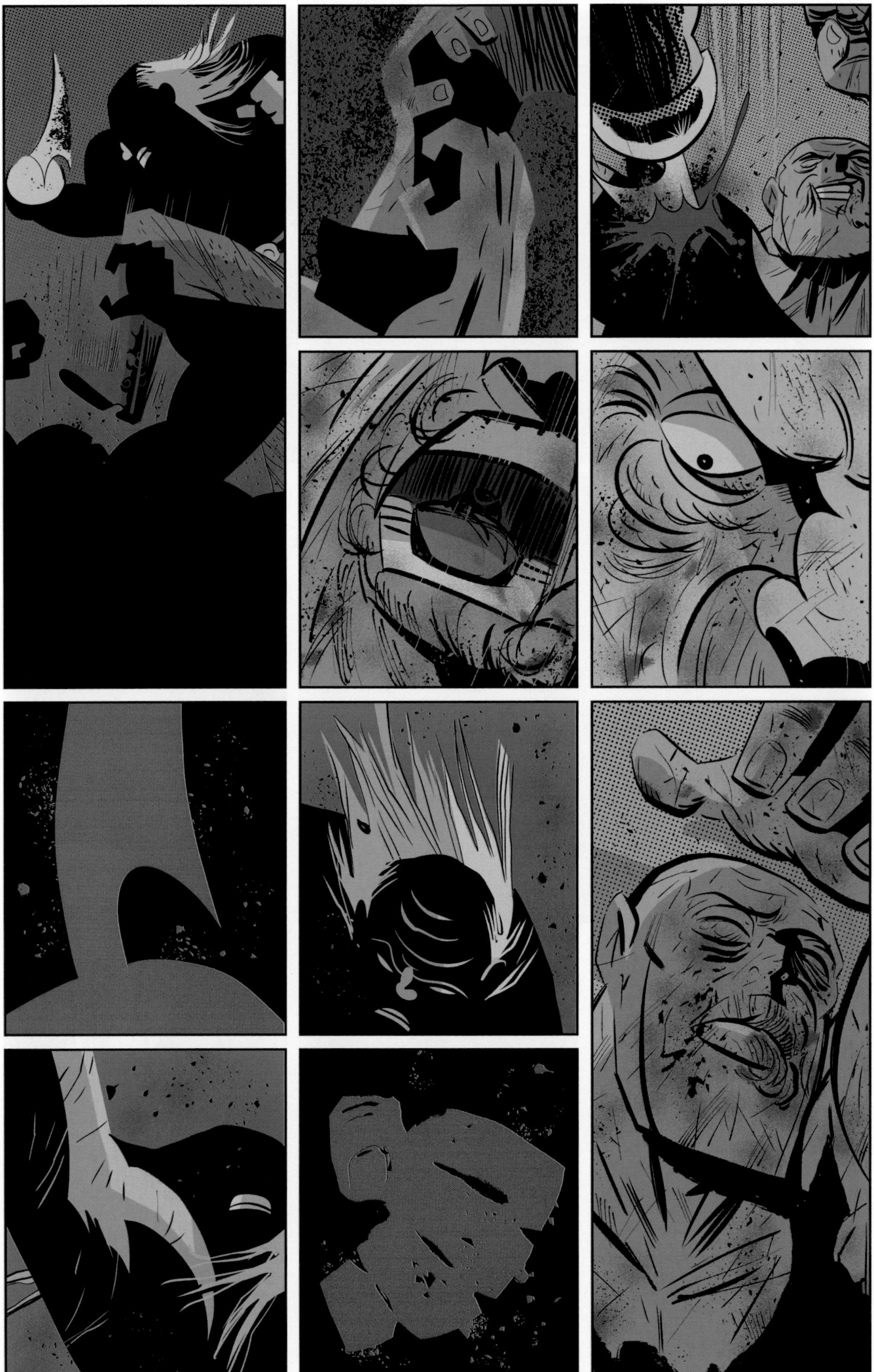

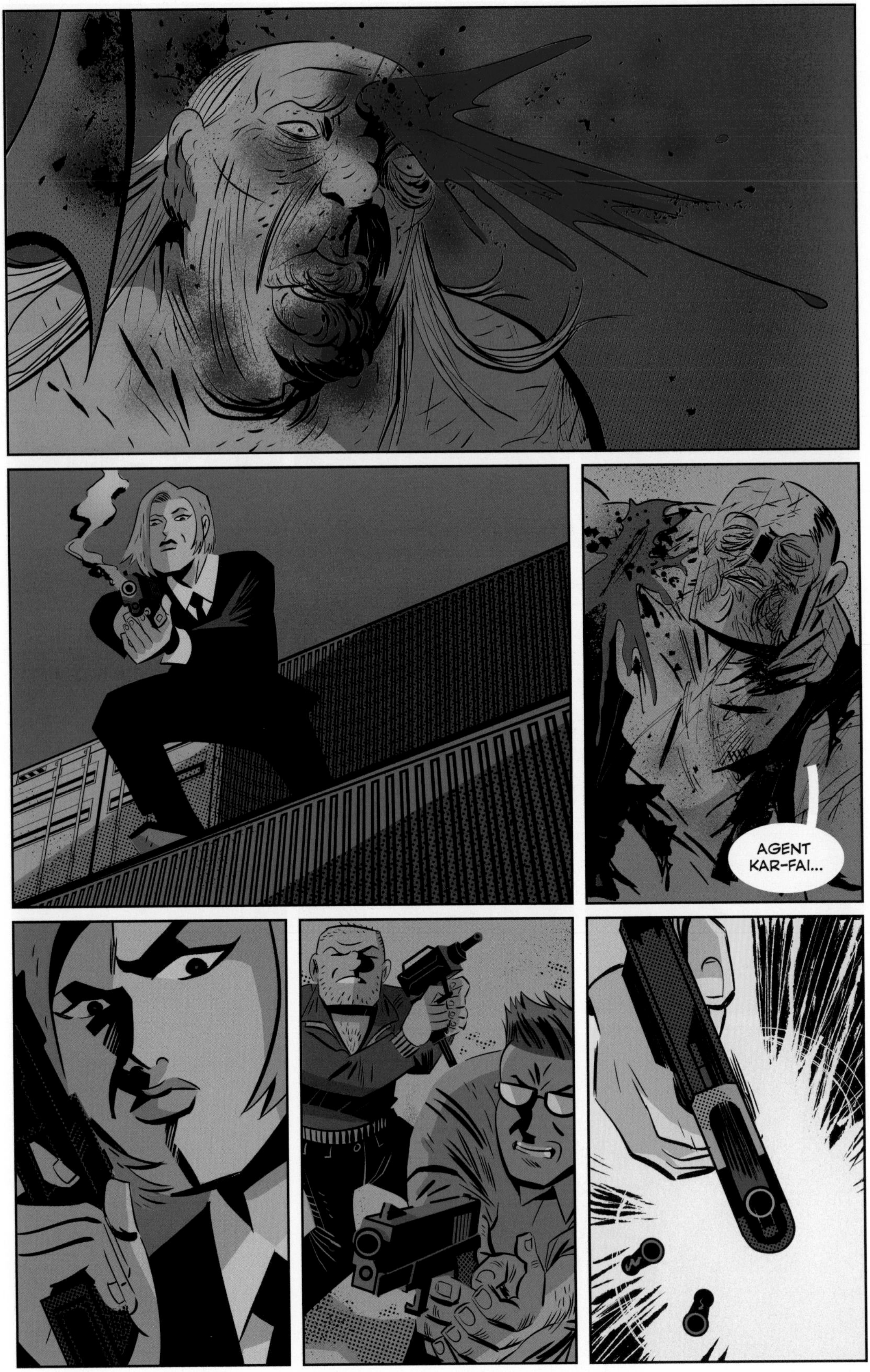
AGENT KAR-FAI...

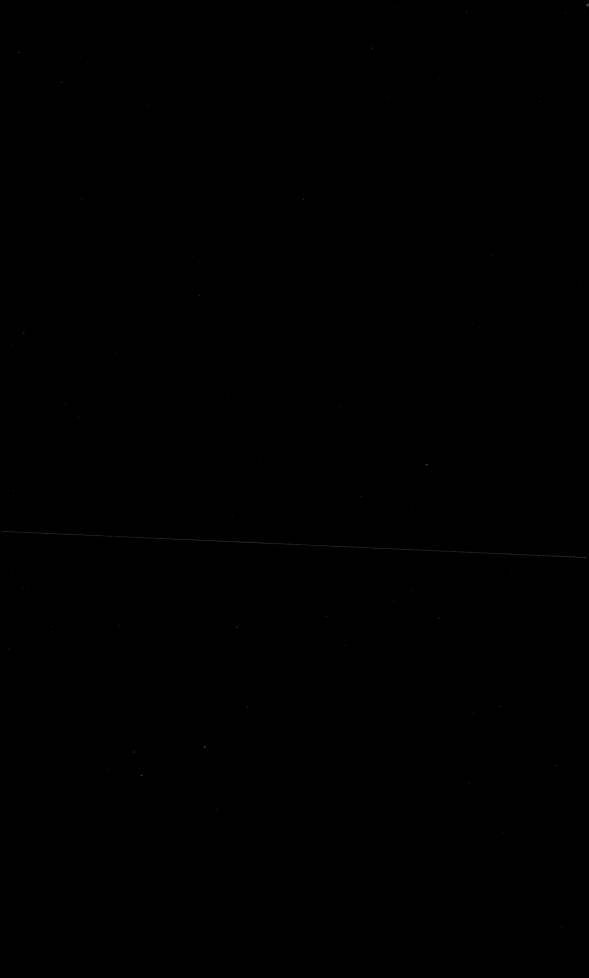

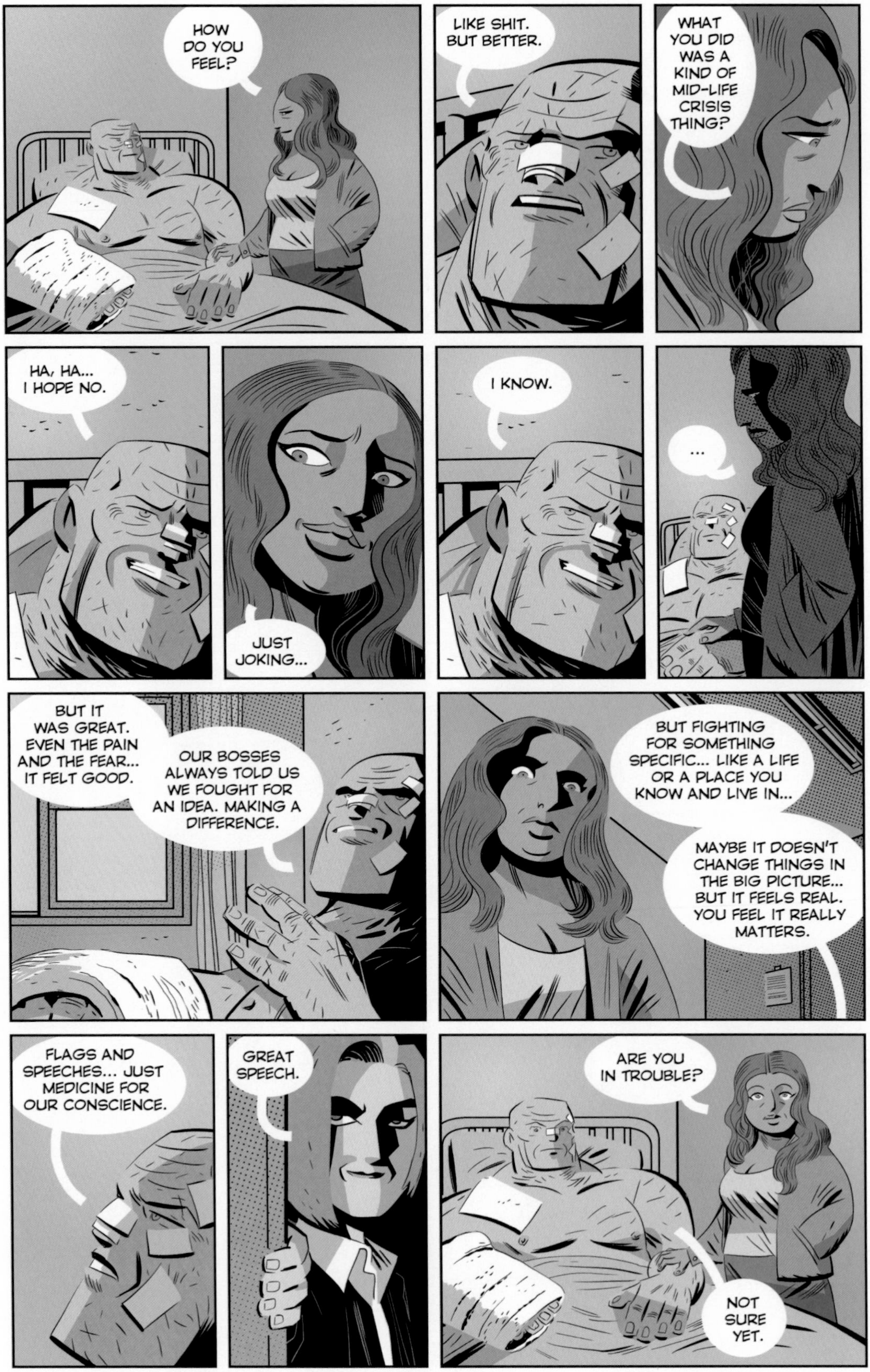
HOW DO YOU FEEL?
LIKE SHIT. BUT BETTER.
WHAT YOU DID WAS A KIND OF MID-LIFE CRISIS THING?
HA, HA... I HOPE NO.
JUST JOKING...
I KNOW.
...
BUT IT WAS GREAT. EVEN THE PAIN AND THE FEAR... IT FELT GOOD.
OUR BOSSES ALWAYS TOLD US WE FOUGHT FOR AN IDEA. MAKING A DIFFERENCE.
BUT FIGHTING FOR SOMETHING SPECIFIC... LIKE A LIFE OR A PLACE YOU KNOW AND LIVE IN...
MAYBE IT DOESN'T CHANGE THINGS IN THE BIG PICTURE... BUT IT FEELS REAL. YOU FEEL IT REALLY MATTERS.
FLAGS AND SPEECHES... JUST MEDICINE FOR OUR CONSCIENCE.
GREAT SPEECH.
ARE YOU IN TROUBLE?
NOT SURE YET.

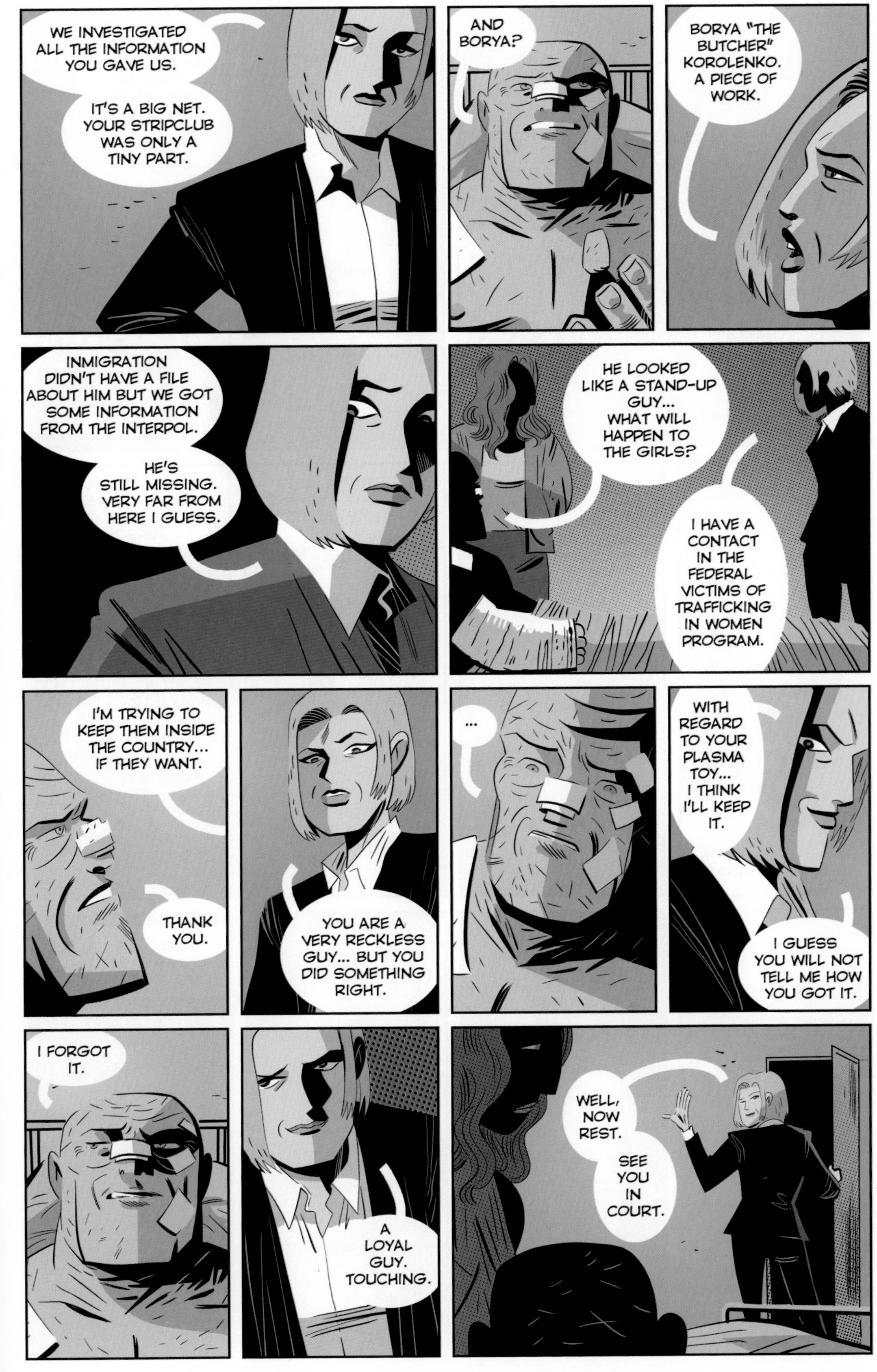
WE INVESTIGATED ALL THE INFORMATION YOU GAVE US.
IT'S A BIG NET. YOUR STRIPCLUB WAS ONLY A TINY PART.
AND BORYA?
BORYA "THE BUTCHER" KOROLENKO. A PIECE OF WORK.
INMIGRATION DIDN'T HAVE A FILE ABOUT HIM BUT WE GOT SOME INFORMATION FROM THE INTERPOL.
HE'S STILL MISSING. VERY FAR FROM HERE I GUESS.
HE LOOKED LIKE A STAND-UP GUY... WHAT WILL HAPPEN TO THE GIRLS?
I HAVE A CONTACT IN THE FEDERAL VICTIMS OF TRAFFICKING IN WOMEN PROGRAM.
I'M TRYING TO KEEP THEM INSIDE THE COUNTRY... IF THEY WANT.
THANK YOU.
YOU ARE A VERY RECKLESS GUY... BUT YOU DID SOMETHING RIGHT.
...
WITH REGARD TO YOUR PLASMA TOY... I THINK I'LL KEEP IT.
I GUESS YOU WILL NOT TELL ME HOW YOU GOT IT.
I FORGOT IT.
A LOYAL GUY. TOUCHING.
WELL, NOW REST.
SEE YOU IN COURT.

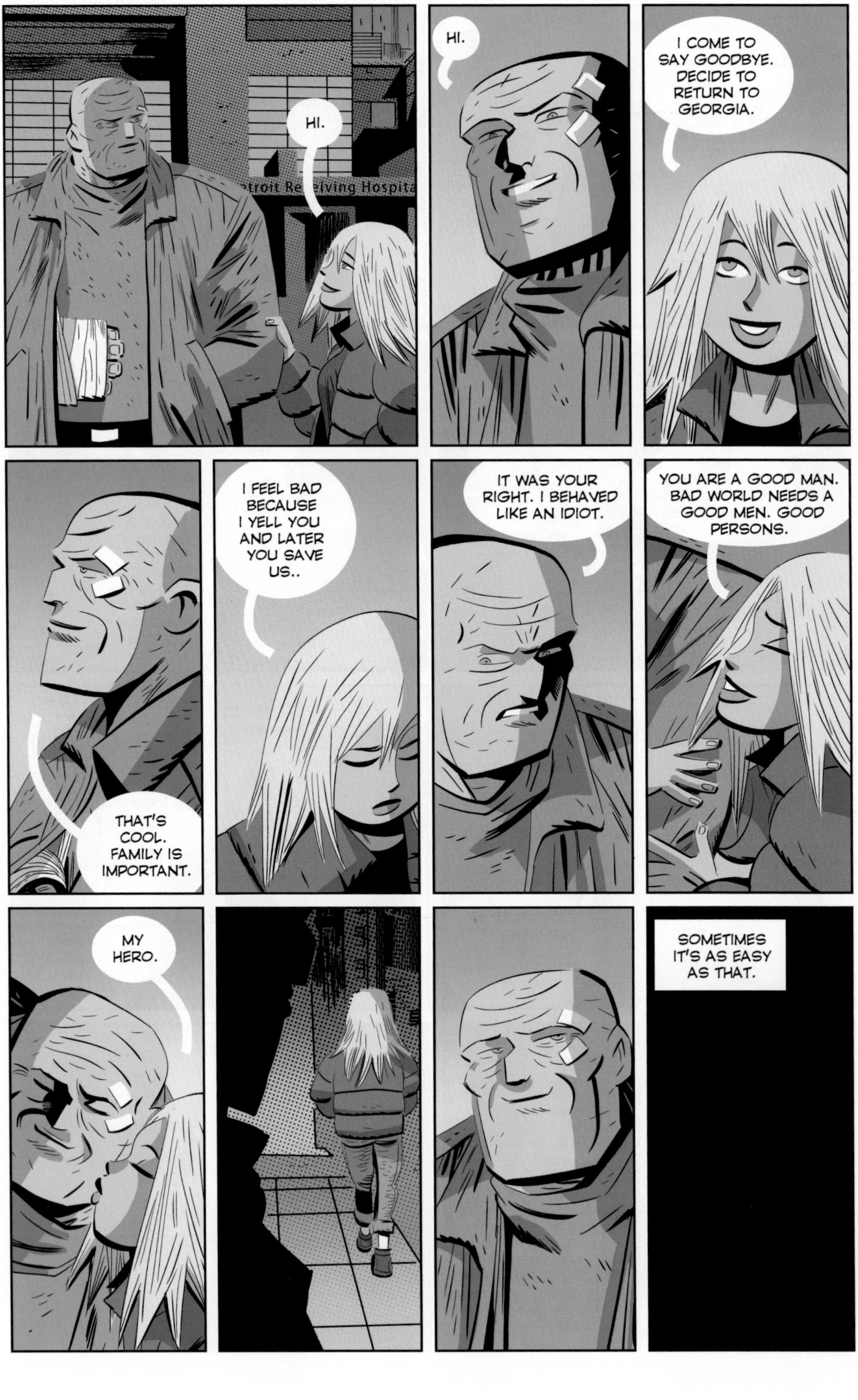
HI.
HI.
I COME TO SAY GOODBYE. DECIDE TO RETURN TO GEORGIA.
THAT'S COOL. FAMILY IS IMPORTANT.
I FEEL BAD BECAUSE I YELL YOU AND LATER YOU SAVE US..
IT WAS YOUR RIGHT. I BEHAVED LIKE AN IDIOT.
YOU ARE A GOOD MAN. BAD WORLD NEEDS A GOOD MEN. GOOD PERSONS.
MY HERO.
SOMETIMES IT'S AS EASY AS THAT.

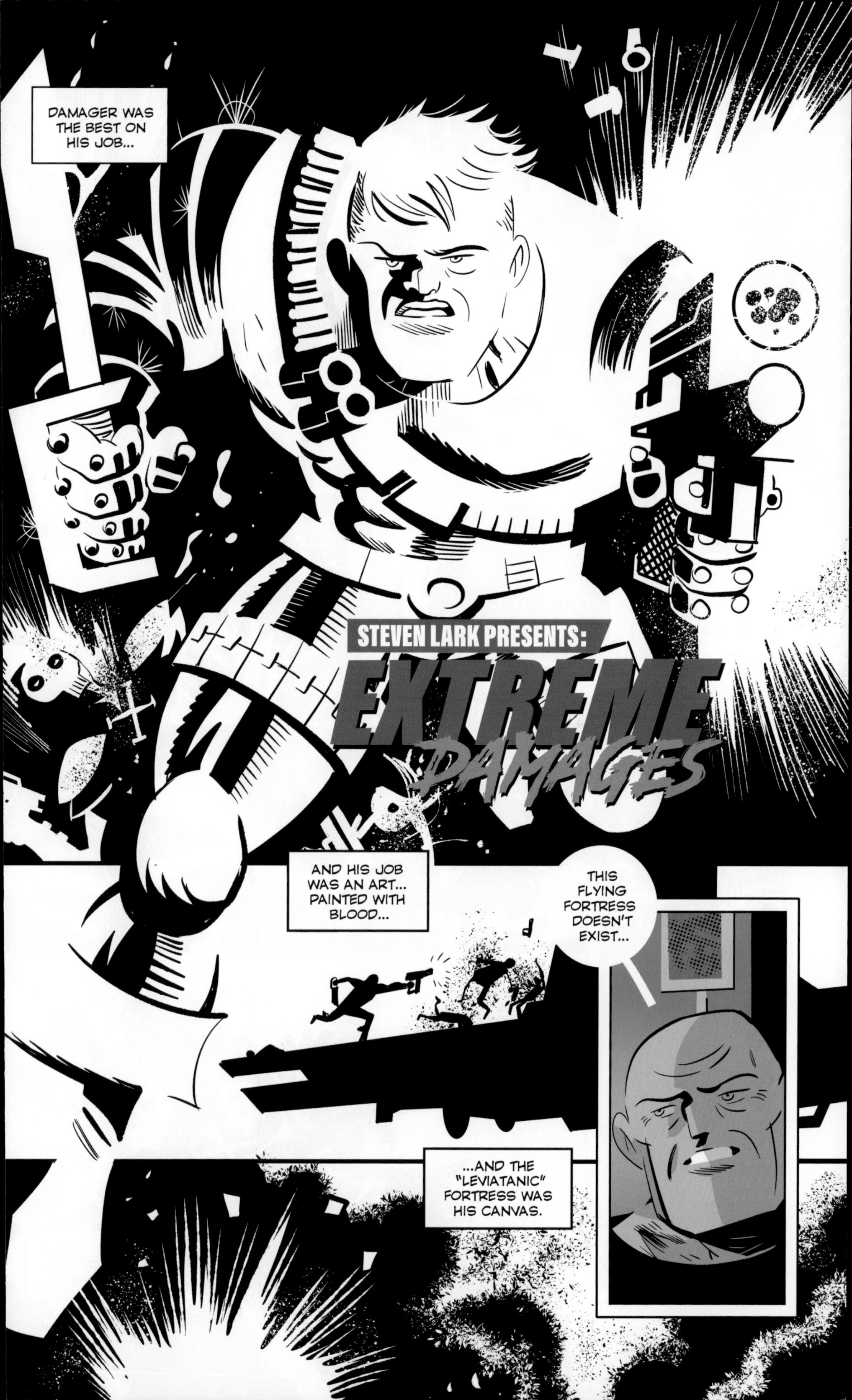
DAMAGER WAS THE BEST ON HIS JOB...
STEVEN LARK PRESENTS:
EXTREME DAMAGES
AND HIS JOB WAS AN ART... PAINTED WITH BLOOD...
THIS FLYING FORTRESS DOESN'T EXIST...
...AND THE "LEVIATANIC" FORTRESS WAS HIS CANVAS.

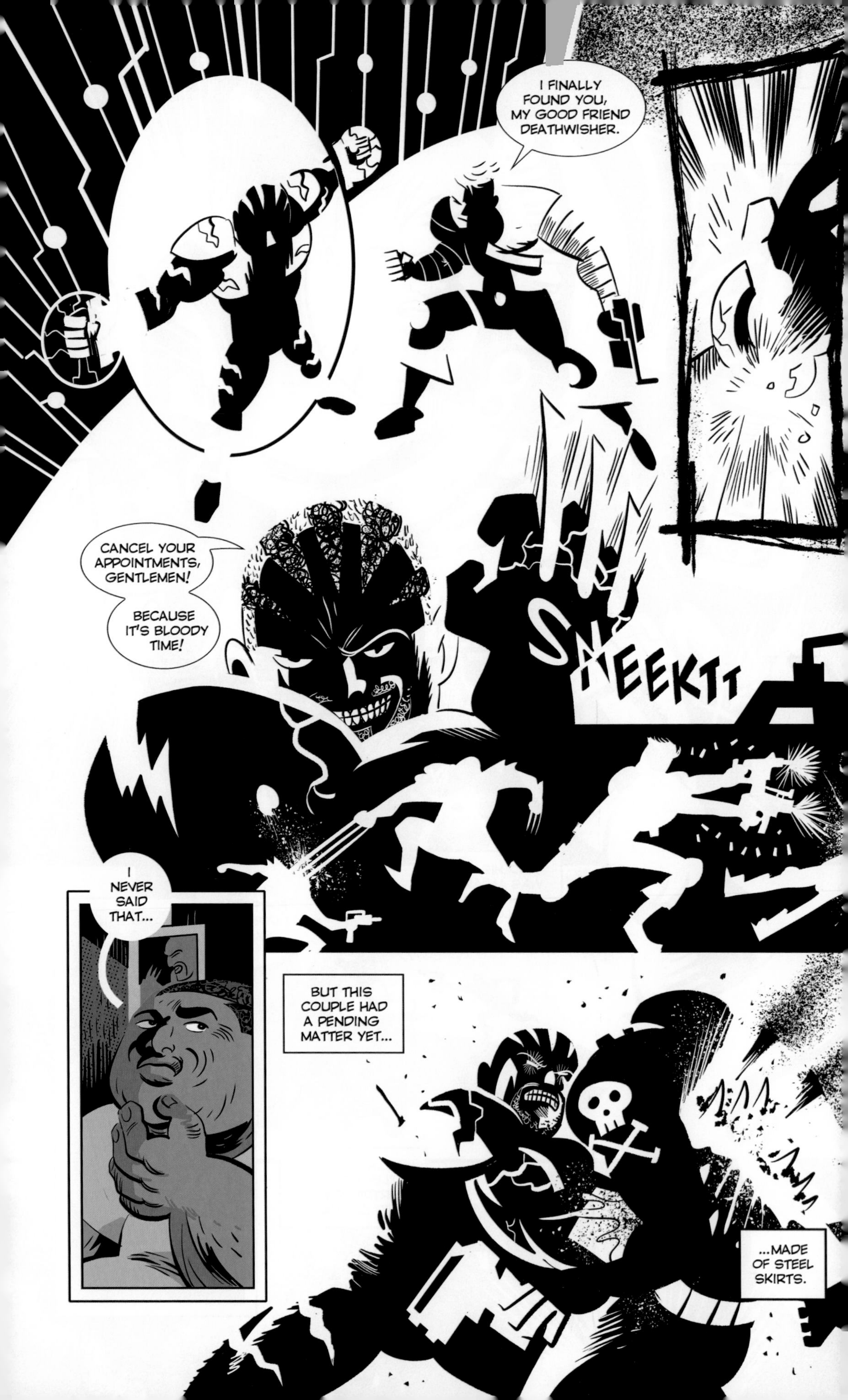
I FINALLY FOUND YOU, MY GOOD FRIEND DEATHWISHER.
CANCEL YOUR APPOINTMENTS, GENTLEMEN!
BECAUSE IT'S BLOODY TIME!
SNEEKTT
I NEVER SAID THAT...
BUT THIS COUPLE HAD A PENDING MATTER YET...
...MADE OF STEEL SKIRTS.

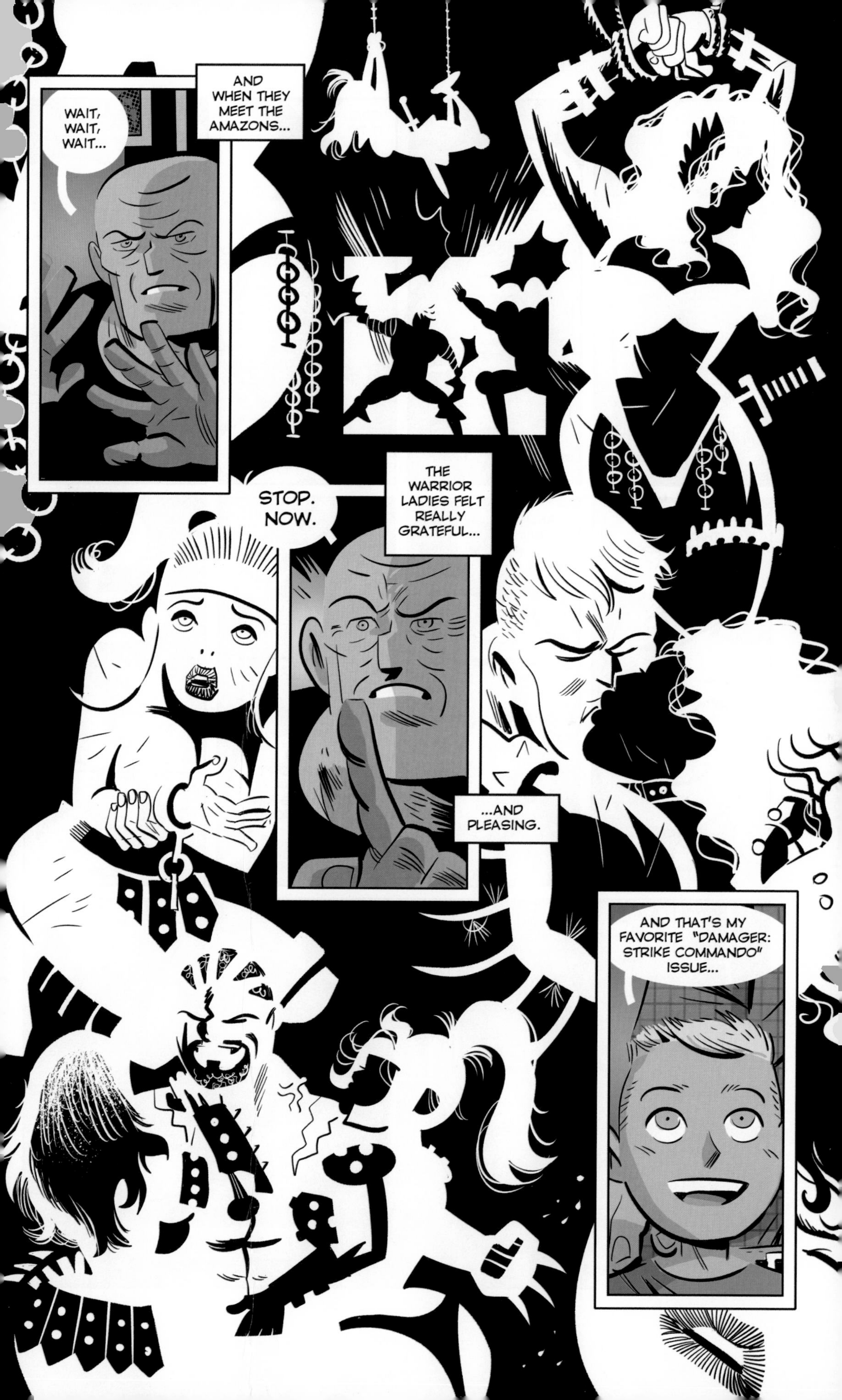

WAIT, WAIT, WAIT...
AND WHEN THEY MEET THE AMAZONS...
STOP. NOW.
THE WARRIOR LADIES FELT REALLY GRATEFUL...
...AND PLEASING.
AND THAT'S MY FAVORITE "DAMAGER: STRIKE COMMANDO" ISSUE...

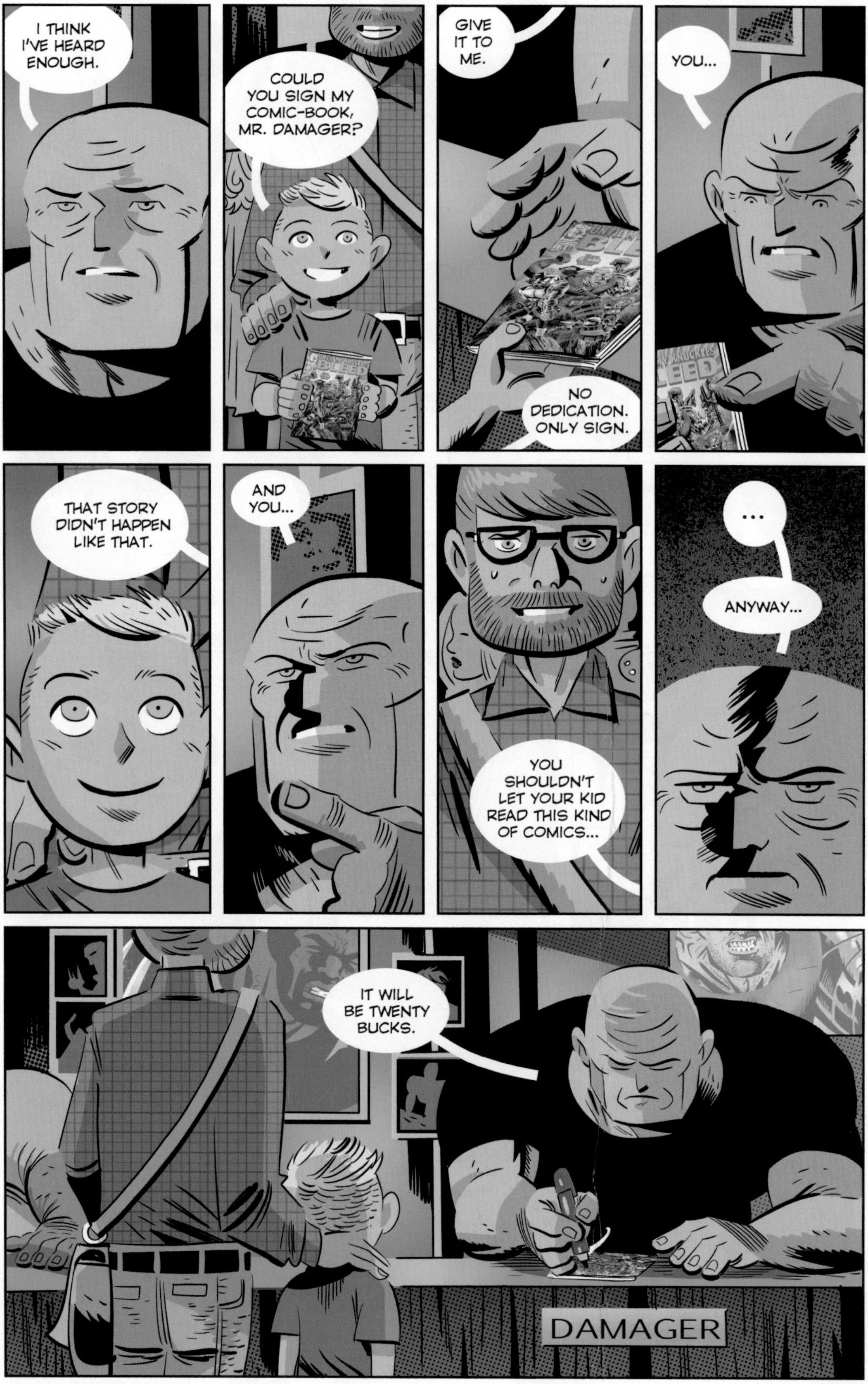
I THINK I'VE HEARD ENOUGH.
COULD YOU SIGN MY COMIC-BOOK, MR. DAMAGER?
GIVE IT TO ME.
NO DEDICATION. ONLY SIGN.
YOU...
THAT STORY DIDN'T HAPPEN LIKE THAT.
AND YOU...
YOU SHOULDN'T LET YOUR KID READ THIS KIND OF COMICS...
...
ANYWAY...
IT WILL BE TWENTY BUCKS.
DAMAGER

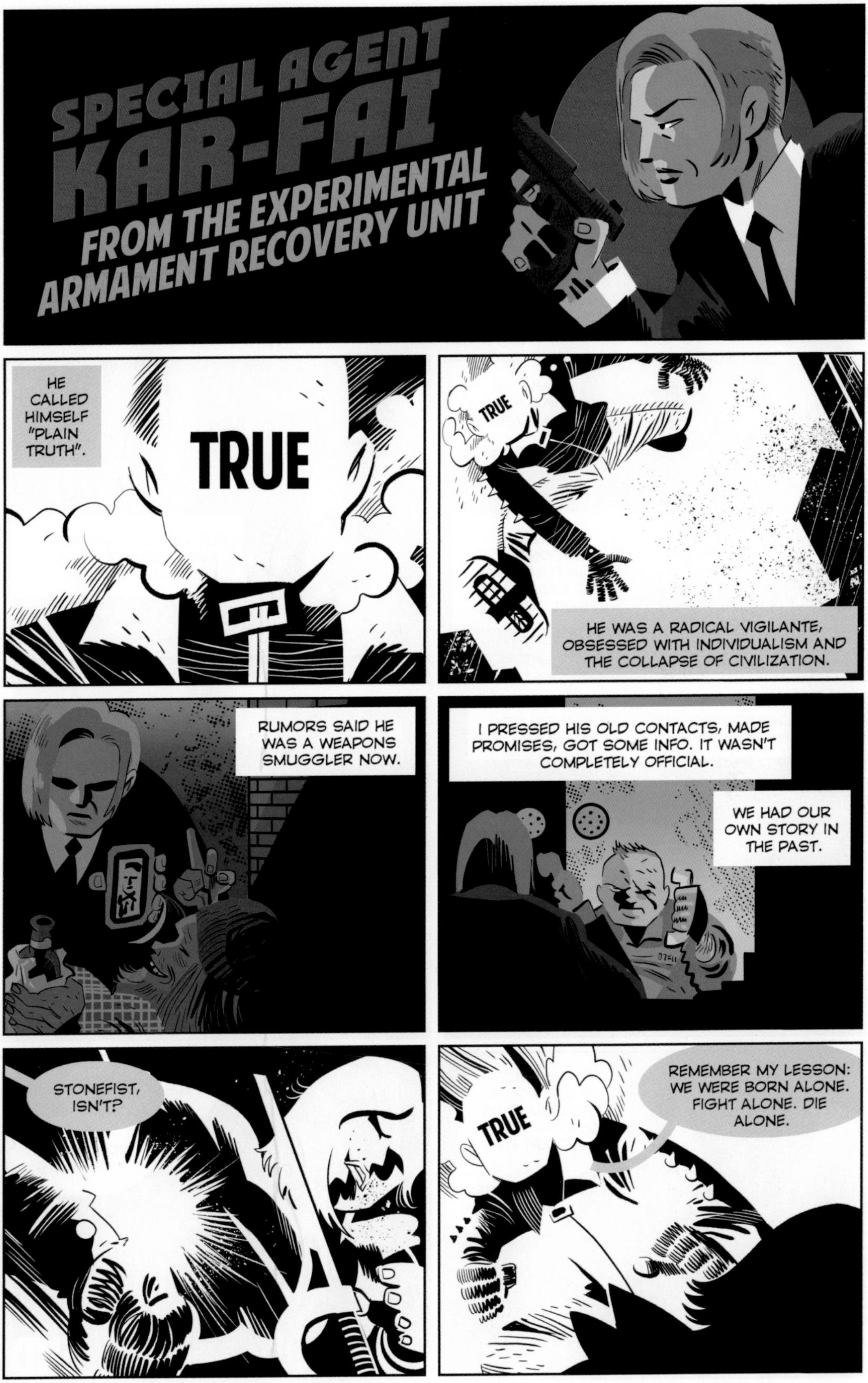
SPECIAL AGENT
KAR-FAI
FROM THE EXPERIMENTAL
ARMAMENT RECOVERY UNIT
HE CALLED HIMSELF "PLAIN TRUTH".
TRUE
TRUE
HE WAS A RADICAL VIGILANTE, OBSESSED WITH INDIVIDUALISM AND THE COLLAPSE OF CIVILIZATION.
RUMORS SAID HE WAS A WEAPONS SMUGGLER NOW.
I PRESSED HIS OLD CONTACTS, MADE PROMISES, GOT SOME INFO. IT WASN'T COMPLETELY OFFICIAL.
WE HAD OUR OWN STORY IN THE PAST.
STONEFIST, ISN'T?
TRUE
REMEMBER MY LESSON: WE WERE BORN ALONE. FIGHT ALONE. DIE ALONE.

I EVENTUALLY FOUND THE RIGHT TRACE.

HIS WAR WAS NOW IN THE INTERNET FORUMS.

BUT HE WAS BARELY A TROLL.

THE WEAPONS WERE IN FULL VIEW, HIS APOCALYPTIC SAFEGUARD....

BUT WITHOUT THE PROPER MAINTENANCE... IT WAS USELESS JUNK.

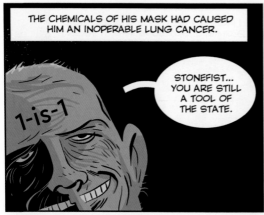

THE CHEMICALS OF HIS MASK HAD CAUSED HIM AN INOPERABLE LUNG CANCER.

STONEFIST... YOU ARE STILL A TOOL OF THE STATE.

HE COULDN'T AFFORD A TREATMENT... AND HE HAD GIVEN UP.

IF THE PRICE OF INDIVIDUAL FREEDOM IS MY DEATH... I CAN ACCEPT IT.

REMEMBER MY LESSON.

BORN ALONE, FIGHT ALONE, DIE ALONE.

YOU GOT IT. CONGRATS.

END

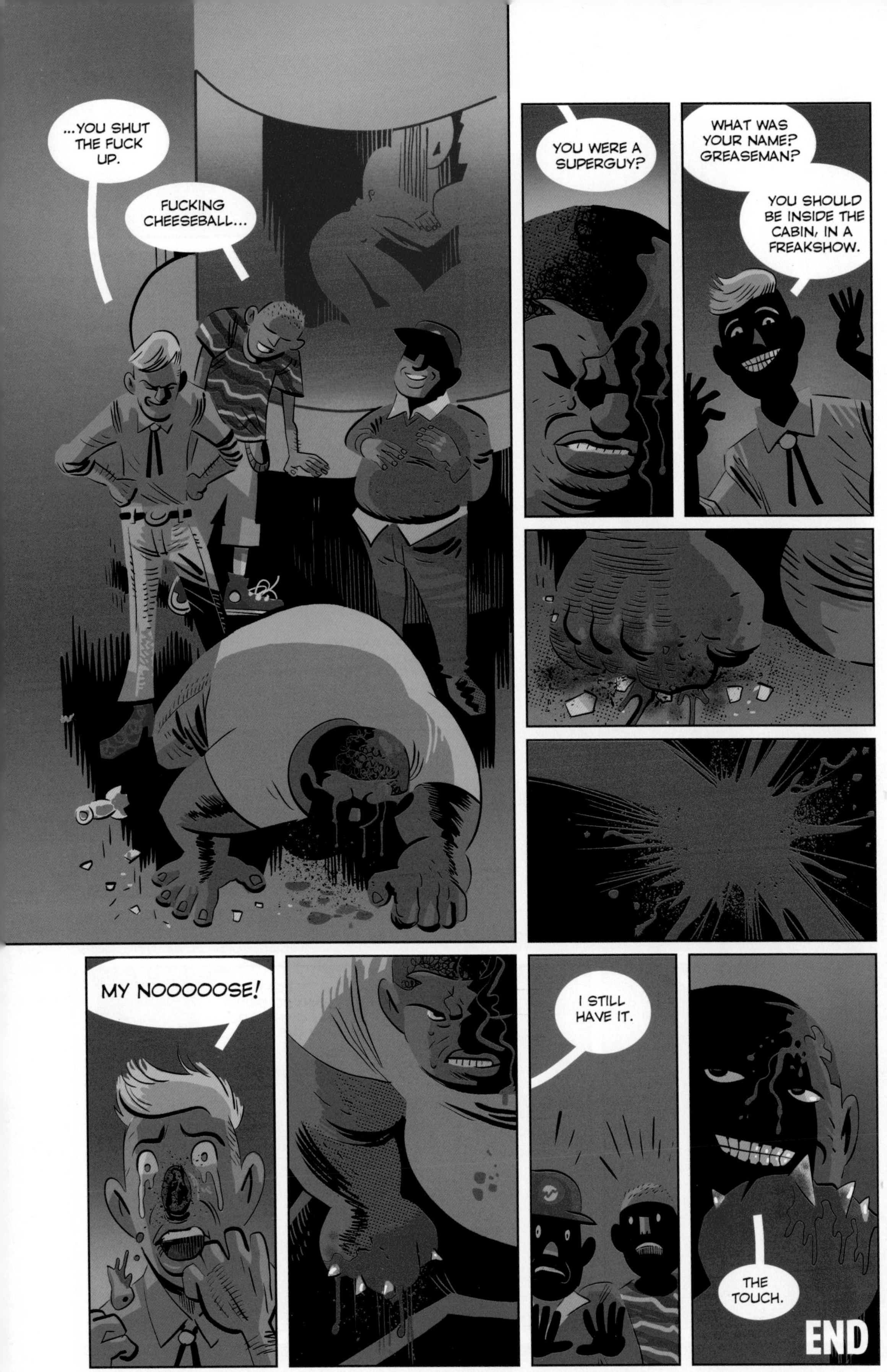

...YOU SHUT THE FUCK UP.
FUCKING CHEESEBALL...
YOU WERE A SUPERGUY?
WHAT WAS YOUR NAME? GREASEMAN?
YOU SHOULD BE INSIDE THE CABIN, IN A FREAKSHOW.
MY NOOOOOSE!
I STILL HAVE IT.
THE TOUCH.
END

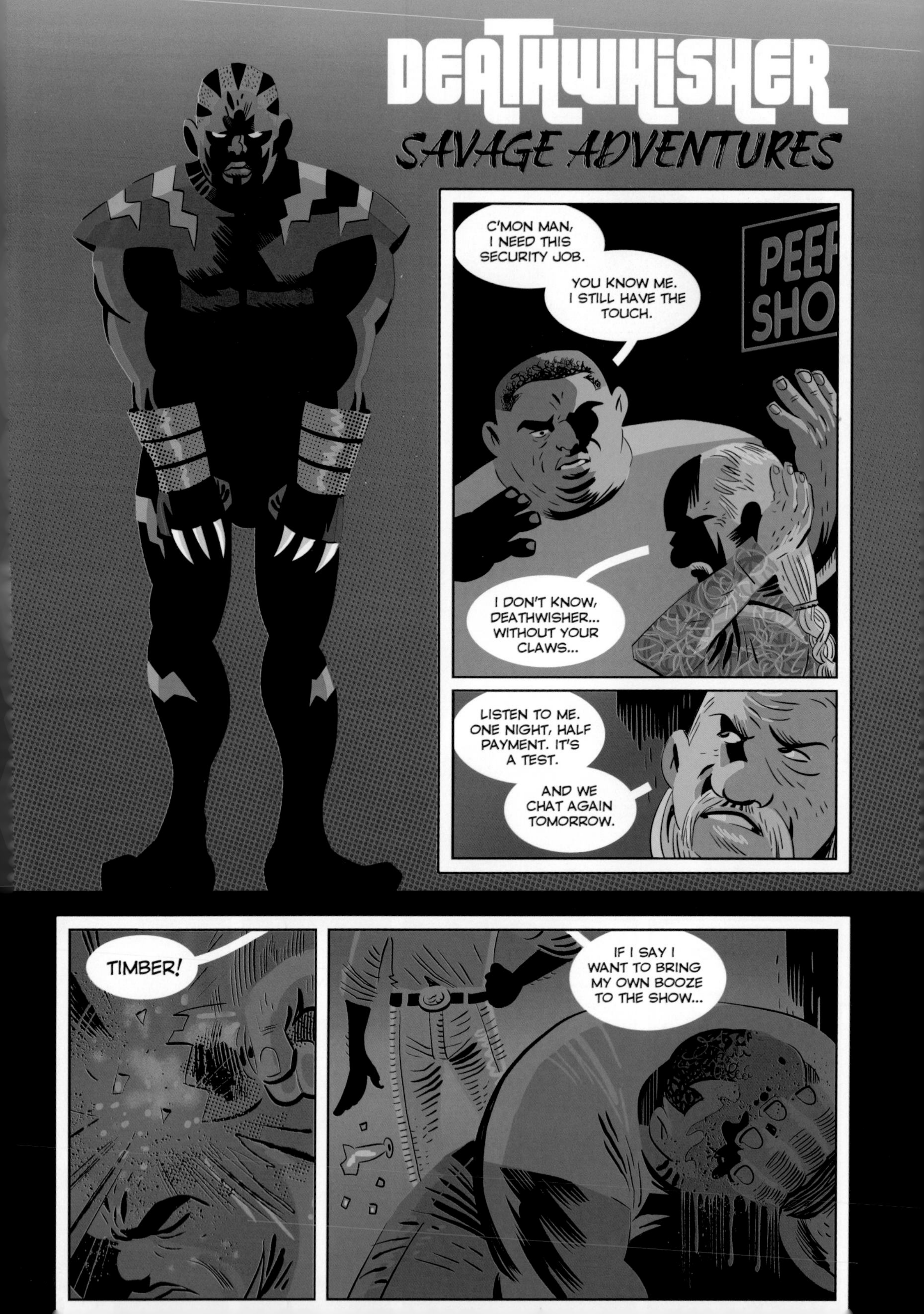
DEATHWHISHER
SAVAGE ADVENTURES
C'MON MAN, I NEED THIS SECURITY JOB.
YOU KNOW ME. I STILL HAVE THE TOUCH.
PEEP SHO
I DON'T KNOW, DEATHWISHER... WITHOUT YOUR CLAWS...
LISTEN TO ME. ONE NIGHT, HALF PAYMENT. IT'S A TEST.
AND WE CHAT AGAIN TOMORROW.
TIMBER!
IF I SAY I WANT TO BRING MY OWN BOOZE TO THE SHOW...